Dancing
With
Demons
A Love Story

ADVANCE PRAISE FOR DANCING WITH DEMONS

"*Dancing With Demons* is a lyrical and luminous memoir by Laura Holloway that grapples with profound questions such as:

How do we honor this precious gift of being human and the brief time we have on earth?

What if we are among those whose hearts break with the pain of the world and have loved and lost one too many times?

What if we have walked through the fires of life, intimately knowing what it's like to dance with our darkness, yet sometimes wondering if it will swallow us whole?

A book for sensitive souls, big-feeling beings, animal rescuers, and lovers of the natural world, with remarkable emotional depth, Holloway pays poetic tribute to the exquisite beauty of life and the heartache of love, inviting us on an intimate journey through her own explorations and struggles.

By the final pages of *Dancing with Demons*, we embrace Laura's reminder that life's challenges do not get wrapped up in pretty packages but rather they come together and fall apart over and over again. And, dancing with *that* is the true mystery of life."

—**Kristen Moeller**, MS, literary agent, and author of
What Are You Waiting For? and *Phoenix Rising: Stories of Remarkable Women Walking through Fire*

"*Dancing With Demons* is quite possibly the most intimate look into someone's life I've ever read. Told with heart-cracked-open honesty, Holloway draws you into the tiny world of her internal life and makes it feel as big as a universe. I laughed, I cried, and I saw the most private version of myself reflected back. Who knew dancing with demons could be so thrilling."

—**Laura Thomas,** author of
The Magic of Well-Being

ADVANCE PRAISE FOR DANCING WITH DEMONS

It has been said that "one person's story is someone else's survival guide."

In craftly resurrecting personal memories for the sake of journeying through and towards her own healing, Laura Holloway has released the essence of what it truly means to walk your walk and talk your talk.

Just like in breathwork and meditation, it is the space between the exhale and the inhale that you surrender to the silence within. Where you are invited into universality, where all the answers reside.

As expressed within, "The pauses are stopping points for the moment, before continuing toward eternity." One question to ask yourself is, "what is truly holding me back from becoming the person I KNOW I Am?"

Laura's *Dancing with Demons: A Love Story* will inspire you to fuel the fires of courage and bravery within (and with-out) you, so that you, too, may capitulate your inhibitions on a trajectory towards your own true self-authenticity.

—**Danny Scott**, Energy wellness facilitator, Intuitive communication specialist, messenger

Dancing With Demons
A Love Story

by

Laura L. Holloway

Storytellers Publishing
Colorado, USA

Storytellers Publishing
An imprint of Journey Institute Press,
a division of 50 in 52 Journey, Inc.
journeyinstitutepress.org

Library of Congress Control Number: 2024939931
Names: Holloway, Laura L.
Title: Dancing With Demons: A Love Story
Description: Colorado: Storytellers Publishing, 2024

Identifiers: ISBN 979-8-9894379-6-2 (hardcover)
978-1-964754-11-6 (paperback)
978-1-964754-01-7 (ebook/kindle)
Subjects: BISAC:
BIOGRAPHY & AUTOBIOGRAPHY / Memoirs
BIOGRAPHY & AUTOBIOGRAPHY / Women
PHILOSOPHY / Mind & Body

First Edition

Printed in the United States of America
1 4 7 9 13 21 39 45 67 76

This book was typeset in Baskerville URW / Footlight MT Light

Cover Art by the Author
Author Photo Credit: H. Mark Weidman
Cover Design by WiggleB Studios
Editing by: Laura Thomas - nextlevelstory

Contents

For Fisher,
my greatest teacher, always.
You Are the Light.

For Nana,
who told me I could, I should,
and that when I did, it would help, somehow.

For Wendy,
and all the freakin' mirthing.

And for Henry,
who showed me you can be a complete and utter badass
and still publish your journals (with brave vulnerability)
for all the world to see.

Collector of Pens

I am the collector of pens.
I am the scribbler of drivel.
I am the organizer,
the lover,
the dreamer.
I am the one
of those
with a gleam in her eye,
be it of wonder,
or of tears.
I am awestruck,
trembling,
amazed and befuddled.
I am curious,
oh, so curious,
wanting to touch everything.

L. Holloway
September 9, 1995

Chapter 1
The Opening

"The most difficult thing is the decision to act.
The rest is merely tenacity.
The fears are paper tigers.
You can do anything you decide to do.
You can act to change and control your life;
and the procedure, the process, is its own reward."

— Amelia Earhart

I came to Colorado when I was thirty-five years old, "for the winter," to write a book. I had spent some time visiting in the spring, caring for my older sister's home and animal crew. I enjoyed myself thoroughly and decided it was time for a change in my life, time to mix things up a bit. I sublet my adorable, high-ceilinged artist's studio home on a goat farm in rural Wisconsin, where I'd lived without close (human) companionship for nearly seven years. I leased my horse on a nearby client's farm, left my cockatiel in the care of a trusted bird-loving friend, for the sake of simplifying. I put my successful Pet Care business on hold until springtime, with fingers crossed and hoping for the best. I loaded up my dogs, the cat, and a few favorite things in my trusty red pickup truck, headed optimistically west. For the winter, mind you. For the glorious sunshine promised by Colorado, which

Wisconsin winters decidedly lack. To spend some time with my younger sister, Wendy, who had said this would be her last season in the mountain town, so I'd better get out there quick. To work in a cute little coffee shop and at the local Animal Shelter, keeping my responsibilities to a minimum. To shake things up just a little, I thought, and have time to write a book.

I had written countless journal entries, some essays, and short stories—my favorite written shortly before my springtime Colorado visit, entitled, "Motorbikes and Horses," having to do with fear and love, and a little bit about a boy. But I'd never yet written a full-fledged book. It felt like time. I was definitely not going to date while in Colorado, I declared to myself, as well as to the dogs and cat. I was going to spend my winter focusing on myself, on good times with my sister, and most importantly, on writing my book.

For sure. No dating.

Little did I know, shortly after my arrival in the colorful little ski-town, I'd be introduced to a handsome young artist fellow, even as I still swooned with the headiness of sunshine and mountain air. I would be charmed by his easy, gracious ways, his smile, his cleverness, and the sincerity in his gaze. I'd be wooed within a week by his raven tattoos, and his bossy little heeler-mix dog. Little did I know, within a year of our meeting (almost to the very day), Ryan would become the father of my future child. He would make me a Mother like the mother I mostly never had, my own mum having passed when I was three. That artist fellow and that baby boy would become the reasons, unequivocally, to plant my Midwestern roots deep in the rocky soils of Colorado.

So much for writing a Book.

The book I came to the mountains to write was my second to go unwritten; thwarted, it would seem, by my falling in love. Perhaps, more accurately, it was merely postponed by other Big Life Occurrences coming up and taking precedence, as Big

Life Occurrences will do from time to time. Regardless of how driven one is to write. Even when one is compelled to write ALL THE TIME, with novel (ahem) ideas of one day turning all the chicken scratches into a proper Book. With mad scribbling in journals for years and years on end. With people commenting on the occasional Facebook rant, "Oh, you should write a book!" With wondering what that would look like, really, and with fear of never doing it, in the end. Furthermore, the fear of writing the darned thing, finally, then for anyone who dares read it to think that it's just plain dumb. Worse yet, fears of being too open, too vulnerable, and people thinking one is weird, or weak, or an outright crazy person. The thought that maybe the dream of writing a book is much sweeter than any reality of it could be. On top of all that, the knowing that if I don't write it—if I don't write—if I find myself on my death bed with all the words still in journals, and in my head…the knowing (as I think of it now, and feel the possibility in my chest) —

That
Would Effing
Suck.
It really would.

So, at least I've got to give it my best try. Though, now I have Yoda in my head telling me I must Try Not. I must Do, or do not. Telling me there is no Try.

(Yeesh. Alright, already.)

Some time ago, while chatting about Life Goals, a newer girlfriend asked what my book would be about, and why I wanted to write a book, anyway. I felt a moment of hesitation. That thing I've heard referred to as "imposter syndrome" seized me with two strong hands, shaking my bones with a gentle firmness. It was a valid question, one I really mulled over, and have continued to mull over since. I think the answer goes something like this: I want to write this effing book because I feel so strongly compelled to write, just to write. I mean, really—pretty much all the time. If not on actual paper, then in my mind, I am constantly composing a written dialogue which never seems to end. I want to write this book because something in me wants to do more with words than just fill up endless journals. My compulsion feels at best like tapping into some ethereal source of wonder and wisdom, ultimately…and at very least, it is my therapy.

Don't you worry, now, I have other forms of therapy, too. So many—let me tell you.

Perhaps it is because I wish to feel witnessed, that I yearn to write this book? In times of epidemic volumes of social disconnect, isolation, loneliness, and suicide rates on the rise…I desire to feel understood, perhaps, just as everyone does. To feel just a little bit seen. Also—and this part feels highly motivating for me—particularly in the past couple years of some really serious Self-Work and compulsive journal-fillings, I've had doozies of insight come to pass, some truly major shifts. I have a feeling that if I can share my experiences with a degree of clarity and articulation, the words might just feel helpful in someone else's life journey. If a book like this had been available a few years ago, I would have been very interested in reading it. It could have been super helpful and insightful to me on the path I was about to embark on.

To be clear: I consider myself to be only as "special" as any other of Creation's glorious, luminous beings. I have not accomplished anything particularly extraordinary in my life, other than in just being Me, as uniquely as every other soul. I've not summited peaks in the Himalayas, nor cured diseases, nor written epic poetry to propel the masses toward a loving, peaceful, joyous infinity. I have mostly lived my life pretty simply. I have struggled, in my own ways. I have loved in my own ways, as well. I have spent my time largely in the company of good animals, and have known good humans, too. I have nothing particularly important to say, unless someone deems my words to be so. With that said, they feel important to me, these words. They feel important for me to release. So, I'm going to keep on rolling with this—I'm going to keep writing these words.

You get to decide if they feel important or silly to you, dear reader. You may do with them as you choose. Books don't mind being cast aside, not like people do.

Also, I will share: There is a memory which compels me from nearly twenty years ago, when I told my grandmother—my Nana—about my notion of writing a book. My Nana was very dear to me; we resonated with animals in the same sort of way, and she seemed to get me in ways no other humans did. I remember one time sitting at her dining room table in Florida, when I was probably near twenty or so. It was not long after I'd had my first (of two, all told) psychedelic experience with mushrooms, with a small group of dear college friends. There was much to be mined from that early exploration, having my doors of perception busted wide open—I'd had no idea what I was getting myself into. One of my great takeaways had to do with the Spirit realm. I told my Nana at that table in Florida that when I thought of spirits and brought my attention to their presence, immediately I could feel them all around me; watching, listening with eager anticipation, even glee, as though drawn by my very awareness, waiting to see what I would do next. My Nana leaned in close to me, speaking in an earnest, hushed tone. "I feel them too," she said to me, "but we don't speak of such things."

When I told my Nana twenty-some years ago that I was planning a month-long road trip out west to begin writing a book (my first book to go unwritten), her response immediately, without even asking what it was about, was "Oh, honey—you will help so many people!" It struck me deeply, her confidence in what she perceived to be my purpose, my meaning in this world, my gift. To her, there was no question: my words were going to help.

My Nana was one tapped-in lady. She was elegant, sensitive, kind, and wise. Her love for animals was profound, like mine. She was a SEEKER of wisdom, insight, and light. She'd have liked to heal the world with a flash of her smile, with a graceful motion of her hand, if she could. So, there we have it. I reckon that if for no other reason, I will write this book with my Nana in mind. Because she knew I could, and because she told me it would help, somehow. And because I can feel her now, as I sit quietly—I feel her with me, and it makes me smile. I feel her supporting me from some other realm.

Now, you may be thinking this is going to be one super-duper airy-fairy read. I have to warn you that it may well be. I don't know, because the book isn't fully written yet, it's mostly still riddled throughout journal entries from the past few years, waiting to be rediscovered. It should also be noted with certainty that, as much as anything, I will transcribe these words for Me. Even I have not read most of my journals since they were written, so to revisit them will be as much my adventure as anyone's.

Perhaps I ought to forewarn you straight off that I can lean toward what to some may seem like woo-woo and way far-outness. To clarify: Absolutely, I believe in ghosts, and I believe in aliens, too (both for lack of better terms). I fully believe in ESP, as well as that animals both read our minds and talk to us, in a manner of speaking (if you'll pardon the pun). I believe we can all communicate silently, if we are still and truly listen. I believe that there's so much going on here, there, everywhere—so much that we humans don't have a clue about, though we sure like to pretend we do. These are all lofty topics for later conversation, most certainly. Suffice it to say, this Life has a lot to it, and that's a fact. My hope for myself and for Humanity as a whole is that we are learning, making progress in our genuine evolution all the time, albeit often with three steps forward and two steps back. Sometimes in moments of laying in a crumpled mess on the ground, with tears and snot on our faces. Other times with leaps and fitful bounds of joy. We're all just making this up as we go along, I reckon; doing grand and wonderful things, or making grand messes of it as we go. I believe that is the best we humans can do. I believe that is good enough, and our right, our privilege. I believe that ultimately it can all be viewed as perfect, and beautiful, too.

Any time I may have begun writing this book in my past, it would have been a very different story. The book I came to

Colorado to write sixteen years ago was entitled *Waltzing the Butterfly, and Other Tragic Boy Stories.* As well as being inspired by a lovely musician fellow I knew in the Midwest (who I often wrote of as a butterfly, and was very much my muse), the title was a respectful nod to the author, Pam Houston, who wrote *Waltzing the Cat* and *Cowboys Are My Weakness,* among other soulful works. Her words had tremendous influence on my heart in my early twenties, with their Realness and introspective vulnerability. That gal can write one heck of a Tragic Boy Story. She also has an affinity for the animals.

I remember Ryan once saying to me in an early session with our co-parenting counselor, "Why does it have to be a 'Tragic Boy Story'? Why can't it be a Love Story, instead?"

And, yes, actually—I agree. A love story sounds way better, so a love story it shall be. A love story about dancing with our demons—the parts of us who need the most love of all.

Right here, right now, as I sit at my dad's old wooden desk with the evening light fading upon a snowy world outside my bedroom window, all I can tell you is what is coming to me. This book that has been brewing in me for the past tumultuous year or two, or for sixteen years, or for a lifetime. Every time I freak out and don't know where to start, every time I think this Book Idea is just too scary, and hard, and I haven't even read *Bird by Bird* by Anne Lamott yet, nor Steven Pressfield's *The War of Art* (though I've listened with ears pricked to interviews with both authors) so what business do I have writing a book?

Then I hear a voice out there—or maybe from within?— saying,

You've already written the book, Laura.

And I smile. I find myself sighing a deep breath of relief.

I hear, *It is all in your journals, and in your mind, in your heart. You just have to get it out there, where other people can read it.*

So, here we go. This grand experiment. This grand experience of moving forward, of leaning in. This story that has become a Love Story for me, though not what you might think of, typically. It is a Love Story, for sure.

I will begin with what feels like a recent beginning, and I will follow my intuition from there. I'll keep listening to the voices in my head, whether smacking of inspiration or of madness. Who's to say? I will do this newish thing that I've been learning—I mean really taking to heart over these past few years—of trusting what guides me, whatever that may be.

I will do my best to convey a journey, or series of Journeys, as the case will be. I will pause often, and I will listen. I'm sure I will mess it up at times. I will have moments of doubt, of indecision, of frustration, and of dread. I will have moments of glory, and fulfillment, too. I will not do this alone; I will seek the wisdom, insight, and courage of those who may guide me, be they in the flesh of human or animal form. Be they earth-bound, or spirits from other realms.

I will do my very human best with what I know in this moment, here and now. Bit by bit, day by day, year by year. I will continue always doing my very best to make up this story (this Life) as I go along.

"No such thing as spare time,
no such thing as free time,
no such thing as down time.
All you got is life time.
Go."

— Henry Rollins

Chapter 2
Prelude to a Dance, or Motorbikes and Horses

**A Short Story written not long before
my springtime Colorado visit.**

An interesting thing happened today as I drove home along one of my usual routes to Fish Hatchery Road, the route which takes me near Madison's Zoo, near South Orchard Street, where I found myself aware of being within a block or so of Drake's house. If I were in this neighborhood anywhere near the time when he'd be headed out to work, I might have kept my ears pricked, as on rare occasion I have seen him in passing, though always from afar. Today, however, my thoughts were nowhere near South Orchard Street, until I happened to glance in my rear-view mirror to notice a motorcycle a couple of cars behind me. With no rationale that it could be him, I dismissed the idea, realizing that it was nearly 3:30 in the afternoon—far too late for Drake to be headed to work, I thought.

But what did I know?

As I turned onto the stretch of Fish Hatch where traffic opens up, the motorcycle pulled up directly behind me, drawing my attention once again. I scrutinized its rider's reflection in my rear-view mirror. As the bike accelerated to pass in the lane to my left, sure enough:

Drake.

I pulled up beside him at the next traffic light with my window rolled down.

"Hey, Drake," I said with a smile. I thought for an instant I had not spoken loudly enough to be heard on the city street, until his head turned slowly, and his gaze fell casually on me. A slight smile drew across his face as he took me in from behind his black, oversized sunglasses, divulging not a hint of surprise. "Hi, Laura," he said. His voice was cool and collected, as I always knew it to have been, his greeting ringing familiar to my ear. "Nice truck," he said.

"Thanks," I smiled and shrugged. "Nice motorcycle." It was an old BMW; beat to hell, and, by the look of it, tough as nails.

"Thanks." He said back. "I'm going to work."

"That's funny," I said, "I'm going home from work."

"That *is* funny."

We exchanged informal pleasantries as the seconds clicked by until the traffic light changed from red to green. Drake said something about seeing me a few weeks ago at a show at the High Noon Saloon, though I wasn't sure if he used the word "good" or "weird" to describe our encounter. That had been the first time I'd seen him face to face in literally years. "Yeah, that was nice," I replied, just as the traffic light turned green.

Honestly, I don't know if I would have recognized Drake right off the bat at that show last month, had I not run into his brother earlier who'd told me everyone was heading over from the South Orchard house "en masse" on bicycles, he said. I'd wondered if Drake would be among that masse. Then, sure enough, there he was. I remember thinking how surreal it was to see him after all that time; his hair had grown into long crazy curls which spiraled from his head like serpents, giving him the appearance of some sort of stoned madman or offspring of Einstein, or most likely a combination of the two. I had approached him through the crowd, smiling broadly, and pinched him on the elbow. I'm pretty sure I said "Hi" to him, or perhaps just stated "Drake," and I'm pretty sure he said "Hi, Laura" in the casual, almost perfunctory way that he does, but the music was really too loud for us to talk at all, if that's what we'd wanted to do. I'd stood beside him for a moment, and maybe he'd said something more to me, I don't remember. I do remember turning to him and opening my arms, then noting to myself how foreign he felt as we embraced somewhat awkwardly. The muscles of his upper body were thicker than I remembered, as though he'd been lifting weights, bulking himself up. Building his armor, perhaps. ("Muscle has memory," he used to say to me.) He held his arms around me politely, but seemingly without emotion. I hugged him sincerely all the same, then punched him good-humoredly in the chest. Smiling, I turned to walk away, feeling tall, balanced, and beautiful. I did not speak with him or go near him for the rest of the night, but was often subtly aware of where he was. I felt Drake seeing me when Dan, an old musician friend, wrapped his arm flirtatiously around my waist, pulling me close. I felt Drake seeing me late that night—walking tall, feeling strong—as I left the club alone.

I remember musing to myself that it did not matter to me what Drake thought, really, and I was deeply grateful for having run into him that night. I was grateful to have some closure after four years; to finally feel without reservation that it truly was for the best that he had dumped me—what an amazing feeling! If only I could have gone back to show that closure to the Me who had been devastated and confused by our breakup at the time, who went through such turmoil over the whats and whys and if onlys of our brief but intense relationship's demise. The Me who felt utterly wrecked by losing the affections of this man who had claimed to love her, but then had left to marry another.

And now, if only I could show the younger Me our interaction that night! If only I could tell her of all that would transpire between then and now, if I could give her even the quick-version rundown of all that she (I) would learn after Drake and I (she) parted ways.

Would she have believed me?
Would she have been able to let her torment go?
Would she have been able to just sit back and let the river flow where it might, and to Trust the Universe to guide her?

Would she have listened to me if I had told her:
Oh, my dear—All is well,
My sweet child, it is true that
All will be well!

Sometimes I wonder if there is a future Me who whispers such assurances into my present-day ear...And if that's true, do I listen to her now? Sometimes she speaks more loudly than other times. It's true, too, that sometimes more than others, I am more receptive to hearing.

And so, back to today.
Today, interestingly enough, Drake looked beautiful to me.

At the next traffic light, I pulled up beside him again; he turned to me immediately, perching his oversized sunglasses atop his head, saying, "So where are you working now?"
"Still my Pet Care business."

He nodded approvingly.

We continued to chat until the light turned green again, when he launched away on his motored steed like a racehorse out of a gate. Yeah, I thought, that bike's got a lot more power than my wee pickup. It made me wonder just a little if he was trying to get away from me as quickly as possible. I wondered just a little how it made him feel to see me.

I drove along the damp road a ways behind Drake and his noble mount, with several, then two, then one, then no cars between us. I watched him maneuver his bike with the ruthless assuredness of someone who has been riding for years, through all types of weather, and who carries with him the conviction that, if this is how he's gonna go, then this is how he's gonna go. I remembered all the times I'd ridden on the back of his previous motorbike, and how such rides drew me from one end to the other between elation and terror. I thought of how Drake would say to me, "You have a lot of Fear, Laura."

And it was true; though I was seduced by the feel of his hips between my thighs, the vibrations of the bike beneath my seat, the rush of air around me as if given the power of flight, at the same time I was plagued by images of a gust of wind carrying us off into the ditch at flesh-tearing, skull-smashing speeds, or of a car not seeing us and crushing our fragile bones to smithereens. It has always been this way for me with motorcycles, as it continues to be: I am drawn to them again and again, but my respect for their ability to inflict great mortal damage brings me to the cusp of terror. Therein, I'm quite sure, lies part of their enticement; their appeal sealed by the thrill of facing one's mortality.

I feel the same sort of fear/exhilaration when horseback riding, and in fact have often thought of Drake's declaration of my fear while riding bareback on my Quarter Horse, Jack. I am plagued by images of him bolting or spooking and sending me barreling to the ground, or to impale my skull upon a nearby post. A tad dramatic, yes, I know, but back when Drake and I were dating, I would see these images in my mind regularly.

I remember distinctly the first time I galloped Jack up the back pasture to the gate and was not afraid—this lack of apprehension was a markedly new sensation for me, and I reveled in it. I felt as though an enormous, smothering cloak had blown off me, leaving me exposed to the warm wind and sunshine—to LIGHT. To blessed Life. I remember writing about my experience that day; how possibly for the first time ever, as the wind whipped through my hair and tears streamed from my eyes, as I smiled and cooed to Jack and felt his muscles rippling with the immensity of his strength surging beneath me, I had experienced the overwhelming sensation of the complete and utter absence of Fear.

The experience was profound, to say the least.
And, of course, not without end.

The balance between peace and fear is something I find myself seeking very tangibly time and again on Jack, as I wrote in my journal recently:

April 30, 2005

We walked, mostly, he being wary of scary things in the bushes, and of things rattling in the wind. We did a little gallop along about half of the grassy stretch which runs beside the big field. I was cautious at first, reluctant to let him out fully, but by the end of the run I felt as though I wanted to keep going; I wanted to go back to the start and let him run the entire length as fast as his magnificent muscles would carry us, as fast as the blood of his race-horse ancestors would compel him to go. I wonder if I would be so apprehensive about galloping on a horse who was more sound than my dear Jack, he with his goofy shoulder from that mysterious accident years ago. I always feel distracted by concerns that he might stumble or fall. Or perhaps if I were riding with a saddle instead of bareback, then I would feel more secure with stirrups to brace myself against in case of any mishap.

As we turned to mosey back down the path that we had just come thundering up, Jack breathed heavily and smacked his lips with content. I smiled to myself, looking up at the beautiful blue sky, decorated with expressive clouds of countless shapes and sizes. I thought about how blessed that moment was, and I thought about the nature of Fear, and I wondered how exactly it is that we can go about living our lives the most fully without being reckless, without everything going to hell.…

Fear is a loyal companion, I find, despite my every attempt to dissuade it from accompanying me to places where I know I would be better off without it. "Oh, no, no, I'm fine—you go on without me," I tell it, but it will hear nothing of the sort, and waits for me every time.

Fear gets the door for me, Fear helps me choose my clothes for a date, Fear fastens my seatbelt and hops in the passenger seat, calling "shotgun" every time. Fear walks my dogs with me and rides tandem with me on Jack, clutching me tightly around my waist, whispering warnings into my ear. Sometimes, if I'm not quick enough, Fear answers my telephone and tells people I'm not home. Fear feeds me comfort foods late at night, then stands beside me on the scale in the morning, chiding me for damage done. Fear scratches absent-mindedly at my skin when I'm stressed or thinking too hard, wreaking havoc on my complexion.

Fear is a pest, there's no two ways about it, and many a time I have pointed my finger toward the door, scolding it, "Out, out, OUT!"

But Fear has wily ways, and often masks itself as insecurity, or it throws little temper tantrums, or it wails and cries until I break down and let it back in, telling it that it must behave, that we can work together, just quit freaking out and messing everything up. And so I pacify Fear; I give it something tasty to eat (it likes chocolate best, of course), and I read it a poem or two, and I tell it how important it is to me, that it needn't worry, I won't throw it out again. As long as it's good, I tell it. As long as we can work together on this.

As I headed south on Fish Hatchery Road with Drake's straight back and squared shoulders in view, Fear sat beside me, not saying a word, but poking at me gingerly. When I had approached Drake's side at the first intersection, Fear had been squeezing my stomach into a tight knot, but I ignored it as best I could, and it more or less let up as soon as Drake and I had greeted each other. Now I even mused at Fear's prodding, telling it to knock it off, that it really didn't matter anyway whether Drake was trying to outrun me or not—I was over him, man, looong over him. It had been proven to me that night at the show, after all, right?

Right.
Fear looked at me pathetically.

Drake had been driving the speed limit for the last couple of miles, and when he signaled to turn off toward the subdivision where he worked, I slowed and signaled as well. A half block or so ahead of me, he must have been watching his mirrors, because his brake light came on as I pulled onto the street. He did a big U-turn, stopping by my open driver's side window. We picked up our conversation where it had left off at the last intersection, and after a moment, he turned off his grumbling engine.

"I'm driving to Colorado on Monday," I told him.
Drake laughed.
"What?" I asked
"I went to Colorado with you once," he said.
"I know you did," I smiled, remembering our trek out west for my older sister's wedding. "I've been there a bunch of times since then. I've been trying to make it out a couple of times a year."
"Did they ever build a house on that land?" he asked.

My mind flooded with images I'd forgotten, of Drake and me standing among the sage brush and pinion trees where my sister's log home now stands, surrounded by 360 degrees of mountain views.

"Yeah," I said, "now they're selling it and moving to Montana. I get to take care of their horses next week when they go up to Billings to close on the new place."

I turned off my engine, and we talked and laughed for a while about being grown-ups and business owners, and how absurd and unreal it all seemed. He told me he owned a building now, and how weird it was to be dealing with building inspectors and all of that. He told me he turned thirty in December, and I laughed about how I'd just turned thirty-five in March. "That means my next big birthday is FORTY!" I said. "That's ridiculous!"

We agreed that age is all relative anyway.
Fear sat quietly beside me and rolled its eyes.

I asked Drake about his building, what he was doing with it, what his plans were, and all. He told me he'd had big plans, but then everything changed, and now he wasn't sure exactly what he was doing with it.

What Drake didn't know was that I had already heard about his building, which was described to me as a small warehouse, of sorts. I didn't tell Drake this because I didn't want him to think I'd been keeping tabs on him, and also because my source was someone tied to his wife, who I also knew was now his ex-wife. For a city with a population of over 208,000 people, Madison is a small, small town, and the grapevine grows thick with coincidences and overlappings.

My informant, Leo, was a handsome young skater fellow who worked at a small pet food store in town, and we'd become friendly acquaintances. At Leo's encouragement, I also began working at that store, though only one or two days a week, and for what ended up being only a few months. Leo used to hang around and chat with me while I was there, in theory, to help me learn how to run the place on my own. After a few days, though, I got the impression that he mostly liked hanging out and chatting with me, and I certainly had no complaints.

We must have first made the connection to Drake because of the whole skate-boarding thing, as skaters seem to know each other in any given community, with both Leo and Drake being a part of that scene.

It was Leo who had first confirmed that, yes, indeed, Drake had married Jenny, after all. And it was Leo who told me about Drake's building, and about how Drake's Volkswagen bus had gone up in flames, for the second and presumably last time. It was Leo who told me earlier this spring how Jenny was "all over him" when social circumstances brought them together… at which point I got confused.

"What do you mean?" I asked. "I mean she's frikkin' married, right?"

"Oh, no, not anymore," he said. "They got divorced a while ago."

I could hardly believe my ears.

It seems awful, and I probably should not admit to this, but I had a hearty chuckle over the news—and about Drake's bus going up in flames again, too. It's terrible, I know. It's just that some part of me felt morbidly amused, and more importantly, somehow vindicated. It was as though Drake had been served his just desserts for breaking my heart that summer, and for going back to Jenny, as had been my most gut-wrenching fear at the time. It's though he got what he deserved for saying to me (as I searched desperately for some tangible meaning in his abandonment of our ship), "I never said that I was stable."

Fear sat beside me in my truck, quietly remembering all of this, as Drake and I talked and laughed.

Journal Entry, November 11, 2001

Worthy of noting:
 The night before last I had a dream about Drake. In the dream, Jenny had died…That sounds drastic and horrible, I know, but it did not feel tragic as a death, really, more just that she was gone permanently from Drake's life. I don't remember the dream very clearly now. I

remember the imagery being somber; blues and nighttime, and an art gallery in a city warehouse.

I remember feeling bad for Drake, feeling his sadness, but also feeling that he was emotionally shut off from me. He wanted, even needed my friendship, my presence, but still kept me at a distance. I felt empathy for him but did not feel compelled to push him to open up. I felt that I could be safe just being there for him in whatever capacity he allowed himself.

Still, a part of me ached miserably, tucked away inside....

There is a funny thing about Fear, which I forget sometimes myself, and I'll tell you what it is. It runs along the lines of the truth that for every dark there must be a light, for every down there must be an up, and so on. So I tell you this: for every time Fear has sat beside me, if I don't allow myself to become too distracted by its anxious prodding, I find there is another presence with me, as well.

The presence, of course, is Love.

I almost want to say that Fear is Love's evil twin, but the amusing thing is, then I become aware: that's Fear talking, and Fear thinks it'd be pretty cool to be referred to as the Evil Twin. Fear is used to getting its way a lot—it's pretty stinkin' pushy, and then there's the temper tantrums and all.

The thing about Love, is that Love does not push. Love does not seem to feel the need. Love sits quietly by, observing all with a gentle reverence, and will only open its vast array of wisdom to me if I turn to it as counsel, if I ask it outright for guidance. Love waits with utmost patience, with sweet and sincere empathy for me, through all the trials I allow Fear to run me through. When I throw my hands up in the air in exasperation, Love whispers softly to me that in this, too, there are lessons to be learned and balances to be gained, if only I choose to seek them. Sometimes Love speaks so softly, so gently to me that I can hardly hear it over the din of Fear, who effectively marches around banging pots and pans together like an unruly child.

Love reminds me that Fear *is* my child. *Treat it as such,* Love whispers. *Most importantly, respect it as such, as children are possessed of a wisdom which we sometimes do not allow ourselves to fully realize.*

It's true I don't have the easiest time with this one, when I find myself acting out of anger and frustration. When I finally calm down and let myself listen, Love whispers to me that these are tremendous opportunities for insight and growth. *Just breathe,* Love tells me, *and think of how you'll choose to handle the situation next time. Because, rest assured, you will be given an opportunity to try again, in one form or another. These experiences are what Life is all about.*

So, next time, will I choose to act out of Fear, or out of Love?

Talking with Drake after all this time felt good to me, and yet I was aware of a small part of me which echoed feelings of times past; the part of me that wanted his approval, wanted him to admire me just a little bit (or more). The slightest inflection of a compliment from him made me shine, as I knew him not to be one to throw compliments around. I remember that feeling from when we were dating, how I grew to where I craved compliments from him, when they were so few and far between. It's sort of a catch-22, isn't it? Because if someone offers compliments too often, it begins to feel gratuitous and insincere. However, if someone offers compliments too rarely, one may begin to feel that they don't appreciate you. Maybe not everyone is this way—I'm sure some people desire compliments more than others. Maybe it's just my insecurities having their way with me when I feel gratified to have someone I admire tell me they think I'm smart, or that I do something well, or that my butt looks really great in those jeans...Yes, maybe so, but still, I think few people could honestly deny that it feels good to be appreciated.

I grappled some with my insecurities as I spoke with Drake on that street, but for the most part I felt good, and secure. As we prattled on about our current lives and undertakings, Fear kept itself quietly in check, and I believe it was Love who whispered to me of how beautiful Drake looked; it was Love who pointed out the little quirks of his speech and manner which at one time had all been so familiar and endearing to me. It was Love who reminded me that it is of no consequence what this man thinks of you, what matters truly is only how you feel about yourself.

It was Love who showed me the intricate beauty of the struggles Drake had faced, and of the joys and challenges that he continued to face in his own life.

It was Love who looked after Fear as Drake and I spoke, keeping it hushed and pacified beside me, singing to it softly:

Oh, my dear—All is well.
My sweet child, it is true that
All will be well.

Chapter 3
The Light

"Still, all I want in my life is to be willing to be dazzled –
to cast aside the weight of facts and maybe even to float
a little above this difficult world."

— Mary Oliver

Tuesday, November 24, 2020
7:21am

I spent my quiet morning time sleeping until 6 a.m., then posting photos on Facebook from yesterday, of my nature walk at Mount Ouray Wildlife Area with Fisher and the dogs, postcard-worthy mountains looming in the distance. I then sent a friend, via Messenger, a beautiful poem that a childhood friend, Aaron, had written and posted on Facebook. Moments later, I found myself messaging with that friend about why she was not able to view it. Gah! Technology—my nemesis. I cut and pasted the poem for her. Precious moments of my quiet time swiped sneakily away by technological silliness. And so it goes, sometimes.

As I'd typed in the comments section to Aaron earlier, his poem stirred my heart. I will have to copy it down in real handwriting in my journal. It's so interesting to me that Aaron and I have been acquainted since third grade at Hoyt School in Madison. In fourth grade we became friends with the beautiful, olive-skinned Antoni, a year younger than us, with whom I would grow up to be good friends, housemates, bandmates, even lovers, eventually (and I always adored his calm, cool mum)... while Aaron and I never got particularly close. There was always a distance between us, despite running in overlapping social circles, and my vague, lingering crush on him somewhere into high school. He was like Duran Duran (the entire band) and David Bowie, all wrapped up in one.

As young kids, Aaron, Antoni, and I used to go "snake hunting" on the railroad tracks, capturing the serpents gently by hand, always releasing them, eventually, though sometimes we might keep them a while as pets. Aaron's family was on a pedestal, in my eyes. I remember feeling awkward in their presence, always afraid I'd say or do something dumb. Their artistic old house smelled of spices and wood, and was filled with books, animals, and beautiful artifacts collected from worldly travels. Aaron's older sister and his parents seemed uber-hip and smart to me, and were into music like the Beatles. They had an African Grey parrot who spoke in full sentences, and a Siamese cat with an exotic Egyptian name. The family had piranhas in a large tank upstairs, and Aaron had a boa constrictor named Mister Bill. He introduced me to the concept of rats as pets, which became an early staple of my affinity for beastly companions, well into my teenage years, before developing a tragic allergy to rodents. I acquired my first baby rat from Aaron, naming her Petite Reppel ("Little Rascal" in French, as I'd looked it up in my Dad's French/English Dictionary—my nearest brush with feeling "worldly"). She otherwise would have been a meal for Bill. I remember watching in horror one time as Aaron dropped a baby "pinky" rat into the piranha tank, just for effect. The image is forever emblazoned in my mind, of the embryo-looking infant sinking slowly, with a pendulum sway through the water. Motionless, helpless, its tiny pink paws curled toward its chest, while the piranhas swam toward it, and I quickly turned away.

Now.
Here.

There are thick flakes of snow swirling snow-globe style outside these townhouse windows, where I sit warm and comfortable at my guest room desk. The wee rat-dog, Ashaya, is curled on my lap as I write. Apollo the Cat and Anzu (my beloved Rez dog, ball-chaser, bosser of all other dogs, and herder of peskery cats), lay curled on the double guest bed behind me. The elderly Manu Chihuahua left the room for a couple of minutes, but now has returned to the bed. I'm really hoping he didn't go out to the living room to pee, as Fisher did let both wee dogs outside when he first got up, before the snow began. We try to stay on top of that—well, certainly I try, though perhaps it is not of so much concern to the young teenager, who (understandably) has other things on his mind. Even so, it is not unheard of to find dried pee on the corner of the wall. Old man Manu is undoubtedly the culprit, as the only one of the three dogs who lifts his leg.

I hear Fisher splash a little with his long, teenaged boy limbs, and pull the plug in the bathtub upstairs. I hear water drain melodiously through pipes in the walls off to my left.

All of my Animal Care clients have been informed of our Covid test yesterday, and that we are on hunker-in orders pending test results, as well as our symptoms subsiding. My lungs feel rather thick, and Fisher sneezed heartily this morning as he was letting the small dogs out, but I don't have the headache I woke up with yesterday. That is good. To be honest, I am grateful to have an excuse to putter around indoors on this grey and snowy winter day. To putter seems like the perfect thing to do.

Wednesday, November 25, 2020
Still dark out. My guess is 5:30 or so.

When Dan and I spoke on the phone yesterday for about two hours (while I churned out gluten-free chocolate blueberry pancakes for Fisher, and he worked on projects, listening to music with his headphones on), there was a point where I said something about my own struggles, to which Dan interjected, "You? Struggle?"

I thought at first that he was being sarcastic, having known me from way back in the days of youthful torment, when we were both just barely into our twenties; so young, and lovely, and naive. When he was the beautiful bass player of a prominent Madison band, and I was the deep-feeling romantic, to be swayed readily by his creativity, and by his charming ways.

But no, he meant it. Apparently, from afar it seems to him that I have it all together, even if only compared to some. It is all about perspectives, I know, and this is not about comparisons, this life. With that in mind, I accepted the compliment, and moved on.

From my perspective, I struggle, and have always struggled, even through exuberance and fleeting moments of bliss. I find myself drawn again and again to external stimulation, though I know intellectually (as well as in my heart) that the feelings of wholeness and satiation I crave can only come from within. I have not done yoga or meditated in several days, maybe weeks. My mind whirrs and spins. I wake up wanting to look at my phone, hoping for some love letter, or confessions of an attraction having spanned several years. Oh, boy, yes. That was a nice note to get from Beorn the other morning. That sure was a hearty flush of dopamine to my brain. But, noh. No more brain-chemical candy for Laura. She must sit back on her haunches and wait. Settle in. Plucking at strands of grass, fiddling with little rocks and sticks.

Settle down, Laura, just relax. Just be here. You don't need anything else—just relax.

So much reaching outward, I do. So much seeking of answers, all the time. There are twenty-gazillion answers out there, I just know it—there are clues, and signs, and riddles to be solved; there are secret messages hidden like Easter eggs, peeking out from behind framed photos of my childhood, and weathered books on the shelf. There are music and song lyrics echoing in my head, bringing memories from so many years ago—the sweet, smokey taste of the mouth of another man from another land, who strode confidently on the stage of a giant amphitheater, singing for the masses like some Savior. His words smacked of seductive promises, an elixir poured from his lips into my heaving chest...*Now, calm the fuck down. You've got a serious side to you that can give the whole world a frown....*

I watched and listened from below, among the masses, my gaze raised to him and glowing. I sang out loud with all the other voices, my smile beaming pure rapture, pure light, pure bliss... *Let your eyes lose their focus a little, let your guard...come...down....*

I sang. I danced. I sweated. I came to realize, with time—that man didn't have the answers, either. Though maybe in those moments on that stage, with all the adoring mortals and me below him—in those moments, perhaps, he felt as though he did. It felt to me as though he might; that I had tasted it on his lips, on his smokey tongue. That it had something to do with Love.

When the hum and whir recede, when I remove myself from the clatter in my head, always I am reminded—always, always, always—*the answers lie within.* Like a pile of sleeping kittens in a basket. Stroke their soft heads, watch their toothy mouths yawn sleepily, their tiny paws and legs stretch, their needle claws unfurl. Watch them rise and tumble from their warm nest of kitten flesh and fur. Watch them come to life, literally—*come to it.* Step into it. With curiosity and bumbling, awkward bliss. The answers are like kittens—this is how we tumble, and hunt, and play. We embrace each other with baby needle claws, we bite each other with baby needle teeth. We require nurturing and guidance. We require warm sustenance, and sometimes to have our messy faces vigorously licked. We require guidance, as well as independence. Then to pile back into the warm nest of our brothers and sisters, to sleep, to dream, to fade away into Spirit-land while our little kitten bodies grow strong.

Light beings, we are, in our little puppet bodies of flesh, and bone, and fur.

I found myself bringing it down on Dan yesterday morning, really speaking my truth. I spoke of my own struggles, and also called him out on his saying that he lives "pretty clean," only having a beer "on occasion," or smoking pot "every once in a while," or taking prescription drugs for his pain. And eating gobs of sugar, as he's told me, and binge-eating meat. To me, clean is CLEAN, I told him—it does not include these things. I cannot judge another person's pain; I can only exercise compassion for the challenges of managing it. But painkillers, drugs, alcohol, food, sex, social media—these are all just bandages to stop the bleeding of much deeper wounds. These things can never heal our physical bodies, much less reveal our spirits as whole.

Dan and I spoke of Light, and he told me that I've got it. So much Light. I told him see it in him, as well. That I feel it in him—so much light and strength in there, so much power that he can use for Good. I hadn't realized that after getting his art degree, he'd gone back to school to study social services. "You are a Leader," I told him, "And when you stand on the stage and play your music, people are looking to you for that leadership, whether you acknowledge it or not. Your actions, your words, your energy—they are taking it all in."

This is why I have asked him several times if he is using his powers for Good. Always, always, always we may choose to use our light, to use our powers for Good. Especially when you've been through darkness, as Dan has. When you've wrestled with addiction, and depression, and pain. When you understand darkness through experience, you can turn that knowing into strength, into compassion, into *Trust*. Those are qualities that must be earned, must be truly learned; it is not the same to merely read about them in books. To survive the darkness, to go on and learn how to dance with one's demons in full light—now that, THAT is really something, I say. The gift of such insight can bring inspiration, can lend true healing to the world. If that is what one chooses to do with such a gift.

Dan spoke of a friend in Wisconsin with a large property that's become too much for them to manage on their own. He said they've talked about him moving there to help with it, to make it a sort of bed and breakfast, and to have live music gatherings there. "And I can have my chickens and my goats there," Dan said. I asked what he'd think of creating something of a retreat center, fully putting my own dream on him. Maybe they could offer music and classes, I suggested, maybe a destination for Outward Bound, or other at-risk youth sorts of programs. He chimed in enthusiastically that maybe his grown son (whom I'd held when he was an infant) could teach classes on outdoorsmanship and survival skills. I loved it—so many good ideas. So much freaking potential. It was such a heartening conversation, so good to connect with him on that deeper level of truth. I felt genuinely inspired as I got off the phone.

(*Remember this feeling,* as Dr. Dispenza says.)

I hear the creaking of Fisher's bed in the room above my head, and the sun is now rising. Anzu and Apollo are asleep on the guest bed behind me. When it was still dark outside, I'd forgotten how it snowed like crazy yesterday, so when the sunrise began to illuminate the world, it was a pleasant, reminding surprise. Fish and I spent the day indoors yesterday, doing this and that. We both began acrylic paintings on canvass—mine, of a client-friend's goat, named Timber. Fisher, of Luna, our friend Melinda's cat.

Fisher calls out to me from his bed upstairs. "Momma?"
"Yeah, baby," I call back.
"Love you," his words echo down the stairwell.
"I love you, too, baby," my words echo back.

And so, the light rises. So the day begins.

Thursday, November 26, 2020
Somewhere around 4 a.m.

A semi-truck rumbles out from the transport company warehouse across the rocky field at the industrial park. This is what they do every night at 2, and 3, and (apparently) 4 a.m. Don't they know it's Thanksgiving Day? Shouldn't they be allowed this day off, to sleep in? To be with their families if they have them, if that's where they want to be? Who knows what circumstances surround these folks, what brings them out into the cold, dark night in this small mountain town in Colorado, in their huge and grumbly semi-trucks. I reckon there are deliveries to be made, regardless of the day. We humans—what curious creatures we are, as a whole. Such curious decisions we make. There is so much about humanity (just to start) that I don't know, that I don't understand.

In my little, tiny world that I've created, in my townhouse with my little, tiny yard, and my little, tiny family of animals and young human, I am a huge fan of feeling Thankful, that's the one thing I know for sure. I am infinitely thankful for the beautiful man-child who sleeps soundly in his bed above my head (I hear it creak now as he stirs). I am infinitely grateful for this beautiful dog who sleeps curled on the bed behind me, for the cat who moseys into the room quietly, greets me with a gentle, meowing *Hello*. He allows me to stroke his soft head once or twice, then levitates gracefully onto the bed. He moves in close to my lovely Anzu, hunkers into the shape of a purring cat loaf, to close his eyes gently, and be still. I am infinitely grateful for the peace of this time of night/early morning, for the quiet of the house. For the words which are allowed to flow freely from my mind, my heart, my pen. I am grateful for this path that I am on, for all of its twists and turns and curiosities. Indeed, I am learning; I can feel myself growing. I am thankful for all the opportunities presented to me—to learn, to grow, to ponder all that I see.

And also, to be still –

to be quiet,
to be calm.

To feel this peace.

Happy Thanksgiving Day.

I woke up close to 3 a.m., thinking about the Book. Wondering how it will unfold, feeling some apprehension around it. It is that age old tale of never embarking on an endeavor for fear of it failing. Well, poop. I suppose if it "fails" (meaning, what—that I don't write it? Or that it ends up being all gobblety-gook in the end?) that in itself could present yet another glorious opportunity for Personal Growth. That, and I keep reminding myself: the stars have foretold of great opportunity on the horizon, that there is important work for me to do, should I choose it. When the astrologer relayed these messages to me, it felt so hopeful. It felt aligned with something in me which resonates as TRUTH. The little voice I hear when I am still; the voice which says softly, like a Tinkerbell of light:

Yep, that's the ticket.
The opportunity is there for you to seize it, if you will. To cradle it and nurture it and roll with it and let it flow, let it grow.
The work, the insight is out there for you to share; to stand, beaming, as those ripples flow.

It is the Stepping Into Action part where I hesitate, the fear of the unknown and daunting tasks—of writing a book. Of stepping into a new way of thinking, of living, of *being*, in the end. Of truly embracing the power of raw and honest Creation. That's the part where I am *practicing*, and sure appreciate the guidance, Spirits. I sure appreciate the help. I appreciate when you rouse me gently at 3 a.m. from dreams of Inspiration, even if I don't fully remember them. I remember the sensation of warm fur, the feeling of Love and abundance. The nurturing feel of colors, of light, of people—no, BEINGS—all around me, gently. Just like the rocks, the birds, the trees. I feel supported, guided. I feel replenished, and full. I awake feeling ALIVE.

So, there we have it.
What to do next, then, in these bodies of clay?
What do I choose to create today?

Health.
Abundance

Support.
Love.
Creativity.
Color.
Light.

And PATIENCE, always patience. With myself, with life, with those around me. Most importantly, with my darling, beautiful boy, who spins around excitedly like some glimmering berserker. He has so much energy, so many ideas, so many thoughts and words. I desire to be in balance so that I may be of support to him. Please, Mother, please Spirits, please help me to stay grounded, to stay rooted in my strength, so that I may be of gentle support to him, this most magical child, this beaming, glorious Light. Please guide us both to our focus, our balance, to our magical powers, upon this winding path of Life.

Chapter 4
The Dance

"Things are only real after one has learned to agree on their realness...Something took place between you and the coyote, but it wasn't talk. I have been in the same quandary myself. I've told you that once I talked with a deer; now you've talked to a coyote, but neither you nor I will ever know what really took place at those times."

— Carlos Castaneda, *Tales of Power*

Friday, November 27, 2020
4:35 a.m., or so.

Very dark outside. No semi-trucks out at the transport company warehouse...I do hope the truck drivers are home this morning, sleeping in.

Last night, just as I had fallen asleep, Fisher called out to me from his bedroom across the hallway, something about Black Friday and all the sales that would be happening (tomorrow) today. I called back softly, not wanting to fully wake myself up, that we could talk about it in the morning. I keep reminding myself that all of this is really hard on him; the hunkering-in, the re-upping of pandemic concerns. It can make everything seem a little wonky and overly worrying, even simple things like holiday shopping...which I find wonky and worrying in "normal" times. Yesterday, Thanksgiving Day, it was so good just to be able to get out of the house, to go over to Wendy's and embark on a sunny, socially distanced walk around their big, fancy neighborhood, with its wide streets and large yards, where you can generally see what's coming around any bend. With our masks on, and me carrying Dad's old spring-loaded, striped umbrella at the ready, to be wielded as a colorful, surprising shield should we encounter any loose dogs. There was one Rottweiler-looking mix who was bouncing up to bark at us over a mere four-foot fence, and I stopped in my tracks, thinking, *that dog can go right over that fence, if he wants to.* Thankfully, the owner came out right away to bring the barking dog in, but I still waited in the middle of the street with Anzu on high alert at my side while Wendy was kind enough to dispose of a bag of poop for me at the neighborhood poop station which lived by the barking dog's house.

Fisher and his two younger cousins played with a small strip of melting snow in the street. It was windy, and we were all bundled up. Fisher had not worn a hat, so I was glad when Wendy backed me up on my insistence that he keep his hood up, to keep the wind out of his ears. My patience had worn thin after a morning of one argument with him after another, over things that were valid from my perspective, but I sure could have handled better. I felt relieved when Wendy offered for Fish to stay at their house an hour longer, as his cousin wanted to build a pump track in their back yard. This was exactly what the boys needed; to be outside, and to be boys. And me—what I needed was to have some quiet time at home, alone. So, that was just perfect. I got to sit at the dining room table, listen to a Rich Roll podcast, and work on my goat portrait in peace. Fisher called before he was supposed to ride his bike home, asking if he could stay a while longer. Sure, I told him, he could stay until four.

A long-time pet care client turned Mother Figure to me, called to say that she and her husband were bringing over some turkey. She asked if we preferred white or dark meat, and if Fisher would like a drumstick and some pie. So, along with the mini green bean casserole Wendy sent me home with, and the salad I made, Fisher and I ended up having a fine representation of what a proper Thanksgiving supper ought to look like. I cleared the books and paints and desk-like clutter from the dining room table. We lit candles and everything, and spoke of what we're thankful for. There is a lot, for sure.

I feel my sadness creeping in, and I do not want it, but to deny it, I know, will only make it worse. Instead, consider the decision to open that door, to invite it in, to make it a hot cup of tea. To offer my sadness a seat by my imaginary fire, in my imaginary warm, wooden house. What would that look like? What does that look like, Me? To sit close to my sadness, to give it my full attention, to lay my hand gently on its knee as it speaks. What is my sadness saying to me? What does my sadness need?

It feels lonely. That part I know for sure. The rest of it is more blurry, confused. It is also so grateful for the gestures of caring and support, of green bean casserole, and turkey, and pie. There is some jumble of apprehension around that gratitude, I feel emanating from this sad part of me. There is fear of losing that affection, that support, of not being deemed worthy by these loved ones, in the end. What if someone recognizes how weak my sadness is? My sadness implores me—what if they judge it unworthy? Too emotional? Too needy, too grotesque, too scary, too weird? *What if they leave it to die?*

I move in closer, taking its gnarled, hairy hand gently in mine. I feel its sharp nails brush my skin. I raise my other hand to cup its contorted face. I kiss its rough, wrinkled cheek, now streaming with quiet tears.

"My darling, you are in pain," I whisper softly.

It will not look at me. I embrace my sadness, setting the cup of tea on a table by the warm and crackling fire. I feel its muscles beneath rough, unkempt fur. I feel its bones, its structure, its strength.

"My darling, you are in pain," I whisper again. *"It's okay, it's okay. I am here."*

All of this insecurity, all of this sadness, all of this fear. How do I reassure the child in me who is so afraid of *everything*? Who feels so vulnerable, so alone, so scared? I suppose this is all part of my ongoing Practice in this life, what I am learning, what I am exploring. To just keep getting up every day, to greet it, step into it, to deepen my understanding by whatever opportunities the Universe presents me with today. To practice being humble, and grateful, for every lesson in every moment of each and every day. To keep practicing letting go of all my grasping, all my anxiety, all my desperate attempts to CONTROL. To keep flowing with these visions and colors, keep flowing with this light.

This light: *Breathe it in, baby girl.*
These thoughts: *Keep blessing them, and letting them go.*
This fear, this sadness: *Keep acknowledging it, sweetheart. Kiss its salty cheeks, and also let it go.*
This Love: *Surround yourself with it, my darling girl. Wrap it around you like the warmest, softest blanket, like Light. Breathe it in, baby, breathe it in.*

Now,
RELEASE.

This is my work of Spirit in this physical realm.
This is my joy, my weirdness, my bliss.
This is the best joke anyone could ever possibly tell me, the best joke I could ever possibly tell. So don't forget to laugh, baby—often, is the recommendation as I understand it. And sounds like good advice to me: to not take ourselves, nor all of this, too seriously.
Just keep rolling with it, keep flowing with it, with sparkles of wonder in my eyes. With pixie dust in my hair. That sounds like a good life to me.

I have this vision of a future, of a home, but I'm not quite sure yet where it will be. I know there are trees, and wildlife, and space—by which I mean skies, and water, and rolling hills of green. I envision sturdy outbuildings for the animals. I hear hoo-hooing in the forest at night. I see a screened-in porch, and a big, open bedroom on the top floor, with tall windows, and skylights, and sliding glass doors. I feel there, nurturing, and family. I feel there, the We—the inclusion of one who has done and continues to do their own Work. The partner who has also yearned for me.

This is what I see.
(Thank you.)

I have no use for chaos. I will not draw that to me. I have no use for drama, nor ugliness, nor meanness, nor lack. What I call forth is beauty, abundance, creativity, peace, and bliss. I can embrace these wisdoms in the face of challenge and pain. I can pull fear close to my side, I can listen to what messages it has for me—I can acknowledge it, I can address its concerns. I can move confidently in the direction of the destiny I create; I can step boldly as I choose. Knowing that this is why I am here, that this is my purpose, to experience THIS—all of this—as fully as it comes to me. As fully as I bring it. Draw in. Release. Experience. As fully as I choose.

For all of it, I am so grateful.
For every little bit.

Saturday, November 28, 2020
Just a bit after sunrise.

Yep, yesterday turned into total depression freak-out day. What a fucker that was.

This morning I awoke with my head pounding from so much crying, so much intensity and pressure in my brain. I got to my breaking point with Fisher yesterday afternoon when he just would not let up insisting that he be allowed to go to the games shop, and I finally belted out a ferocious "NO!!!" which, even in that moment, made me think of Caesar in the scene from *Rise of the Planet of the Apes,* where he stands up (literally) to his evil captor and speaks for the very first time. That scene has given me goosebumps as often as I've seen it.

I gathered up the dogs, out into the car, and left in a fury, calling Ryan as I sped down the county road from our townhouse, not even sure where I was heading. Fisher's dad was completely receptive and helpful, even as I sobbed and drove. He called Fisher back at home, ending up on the phone with him for hours, then with me again later in the evening (after I'd driven a lap around the countryside before winding up back home). Ryan really shined through—I honestly don't know what we would have done without him. It could have been a catastrophe, but instead ended peacefully (albeit tearfully) with Fisher watching *Kubo and the Two Strings* in the living room with the volume turned down very reasonably low. With me passing out from sheer exhaustion in the guest room—once Dad's bedroom—and *feeling* that it was Dad's bedroom, even though (mostly) all of my things now fill it. There remains the Amish nightstand that used to be his, used to be in the very same place, only next to *his* bed.

When the movie was over, Fisher came into the room to wake me gently, asking if I wanted to sleep here or up in my room. I wasn't sure. I felt both entranced and haunted by the image in my mind of Dad curled here, just like I was; curled upon his own bed. Curled in his sadness, his loneliness, his despair; knowing that the cancer would take him sooner rather than later. I took a photograph of him there once, when I'd come to visit and found him sleeping. I remember he looked so small and vulnerable, like a child. It was confusing, and heartbreaking, to see him like that, almost too much for me to bear. I did not wake him; I took a photo instead, and quietly left.

"I want to go to my room," I told Fisher, softly. My room which had been Dad's office. My room where he had never slept, nor lay sobbing. My room where he had never died.

Fisher took my hand sweetly, helped me from under the quilt on the guest bed, and led me out of the room. I felt worn and weary as I climbed the stairs with great effort, feeling again like my dad. But when I climbed into my own bed (ironically, the very same mattress Dad had been curled upon) I felt a tremendous sense of relief, I felt the different energy of my room. Fisher and I exchanged good nights and I love you's. I'm sure within moments, I was asleep.

This morning, with all the pressure in my head, I woke up at 4 a.m., though I tried to keep myself sleeping until 5. I still felt like crying, my head still pounding, but at least Fisher and I had gone to sleep on good terms. This stuff is hard, there's no two ways about it. This stuff of being a teenager, and of being a mother, and of doing it all in crazy pandemic times. These are challenging days to navigate, for sure. I feel grateful for the support that got us through yesterday. I feel confident that we will get through today, as well.

Yesterday I opened up my computer, thinking I would work on the Book. Instead, the computer crashed and burned, as it has been threatening to do for some time. It seemed to be laughing, "No book today!" I called up my dear friend of thirty years, in Tucson, feeling helpless to go online and look for a new computer myself. Lee is well-versed in these sorts of things, taking the task on without hesitation. I told him that he is like my Guardian Angel, asking if it's okay for me to think of him that way. Lee said, yes, he is comfortable with that. He texted last night as I lay in bed sobbing, with a computer for me to approve. He then told me it was on its way. Another great relief, and another great reminder—that I am supported, I am loved. I do not have to do this all alone.

There is a chipmunk with half a tail, whom Fisher named Carl, outside the guest room window again as I write. He is fat with fluff and bird seed offerings. It makes me happy to see him thrive.

Sunday, November 29, 2020
Probably close to 5 a.m.

All these interesting choices in Life.

I feel a bit of anxiety this morning, a little flutter in my gut that I am paying attention to. I reached out to Beorn very briefly yesterday, just letting him know our Covid tests had come back negative. He replied quickly, asking if I wanted to go for a walk today. His messages were brief, so I tried not to be overly wordy myself, as I can tend to be. It seems we have agreed to meet at the wildlife area at noon today, while Fisher is over at Wendy's house, working on the pump track with his cousin. I hopped on the scale this morning and registered at about 20 pounds more of me to love than I am comfortable with. This is an interesting place to be coming from when I am scheduled to meet the uber-workout dude for a nature walk—the one who sent me a photo of himself shirtless and, swear to God, looking like the Hugh Jackman version of the Wolverine. (Oh, my, how my heart does flutter for the Wolverine.) The one who declares himself to be very "average" in looks (feigned modesty? Fishing for compliments?), also boasting that he can do the splits. The fellow who writes to me of honesty, while in the back of my mind I consider stories filtered through our small-town grapevine, of other women and their interactions with him—cautionary tales, though I'm sure well-intentioned in their delivery, still probably none of my business. I can't help but wonder what both sides of those stories might be.

Bottom line, I tell myself, is that this is an exploratory mission, a "getting to know you" kind of nature walk. There are no expectations, only an opportunity to talk with this fellow whom I've seen around for many years, and have never been quite sure what to make of. He has said in past messages that he hopes to become "true friends," no longer mere acquaintances. I will focus on that element of conversation and intention. I will set all the curious speak of desire and attraction on the back burner, to bring forward for future consideration, should it seem called for, prudent, and fit. A simmering sauce to drizzle on top, should the main course prove to be of worthy flavor, and sustenance.

Here we go again, Laura; easy does it, and steady as she goes. I am aware and acknowledge once again that the sauce alone is not what I truly desire, though I may crave it. It is the entire delicious meal that I am prepared to settle in and await.

Then there is Dan, in our hometown, who seems to surround himself with chaos and drama that I want no part of. From his "crazy meth-head" friend whom he says he tries to take care of, to his alcoholic drummer, and heaven knows who else in his scene. I want no part of all that, thank you very much. It all sends shivers down my spine. I will keep it far, far away from my child and myself, thank you, though he writes that I make him feel so happy. He says there's a lot of intensity he's dealing with, and that he's not trying to blow me off. He'll call tomorrow, he says, then I hear nothing from him. The next little snippets I get are that he wants to come see me, to spend time with me "soon" (a reoccurring theme from him). He says that Madison "needs a reset." But I have told him already, and he seems to forget: not in this time of rising Covid rates across the country, around the world. Furthermore, in my mind I am clear—not when a visit stood the risk of bringing along *any* chaos or dis-ease trailing in his wake. I have compassion, I certainly do care, and also—I will hold this safe space for myself and my family. I will invite no chaos here.

Let me support my old friend from a distance, if I may, and as well as I possibly can. Let me offer him love, and light, in the times when he's ready to receive it. I do have such hopes for him finding his balance, his peace, my old friend. I do feel so much strength in him, so much fire, and glorious potential. "Ol' Danny Nine Toes," he laughs, after his recent surgery to remove a digit. It will be interesting to see what he chooses to do with all of that; with the powers that surround him, and those he chooses to wield.

I saw a little snippet yesterday of David Sedaris talking about story-writing. He said something about writing stories that have clear and definitive ENDINGS rather than just a stopping point. But that's just the thing of it, isn't it? I adore David Sedaris' story writing; he is a genius, and also…there are never really ENDINGS to any story, I believe. There are merely pauses, stopping points for the moment, before continuing toward eternity. A place to look around, to stretch, to smile, to take a deep breath, and have a drink of water, if you please. A place to ready oneself to move forward again.

THE END.

(Just kidding.)
Bwah-hah-ha-ha-ha!!!!

Chapter 5
The Nature of Positive Delusion

"The arc of this whole business is really the order that we're describing; that it's desire, then love, and then attachment. And often times that people can get *confused*—you may know some of these people, or you may *be* one of these individuals— who might confuse desire for attachment, or might confuse love for attachment…"

— Dr. Andrew Huberman, Huberman Lab Podcast episode, "The Science of Love, Desire and Attachment"

Monday, November 30, 2020
6:07 a.m.

The big, round moon is shining down like a streetlamp in the sky, making the snow, the rooftops, the trees, the dirt, the rocks—making everything shine with an ethereal glow. I awake to see a falling star outside my window in the big, big sky, to feel Apollo pressed warmly down by my feet, to hear Anzu breathe deeply in dreams by my side. And I remember the words he wrote to me, that I would definitely be his delight when he went to bed last night. I remember how, out there in the snow and open air, the field and trees and sky, we laughed and awkwardly hugged goodbye, and I wrapped my leg around him as though I would wrestle him to the snowy ground. How he had wanted to kiss me then, he would later confess by text. How I stood in the snow wondering, as I admired him and his Carhartt work pants jogging effortlessly away across the snow, his shoulders square and muscular beneath his Melanzana hoodie, to his manly truck awaiting his return like a patient, noble steed...

Just wondering.

What the heck has been awakened in me.

The big ol' moon shines down on me as I luxuriate in clean sheets, as I drift through half-dreams of what it would feel like, smell like, taste like to lay my hands on that strong body, to place my mouth upon his skin. What that would sound like, to hear him gasp and sigh and groan. How that could all so deliciously unfold.

The Marcy Playground song "Sex and Candy" slides into my head. I breathe deeply, and I smile.

I love that he's into canning.
I love that he's building his own house, by hand.

I love that he seems a little unsure of himself; that, in his hesitations and quietness, which I wasn't sure how to read, he later confessed (through the safety of text messages) that he was very turned on by me...then tells me he wonders if that was too much to share. Then speaks again of honesty.

I love that on our first walkabout through the trees we were able to speak openly of our challenges with relationships, how sometimes we are "too much" for other folks. I love that all the while, I would later learn, he was admiring me in my hiking boots, my camping-print tights and skirt. He messages me a photo of himself fresh out of the shower, wet hair combed neatly, a towel revealing his muscular hip, while discreetly covering his manly bits. He proceeds to tell me he wonders if *that* is too much, while I, meanwhile, am taken aback by the beauty of this man, now that I allow myself to open to the possibility of him. Now that I may be swayed by the intense look on his handsome face, where before, and for years as acquaintances, I would not. I could not. Something kept me from going there. Now, I feel a curious stirring in my chest, and I'm unsure of how to name it. It is vulnerability, yes. It is apprehension. It is admiration, most certainly. And also, it is desire.

That is it, yes.

DESIRE.

I think about what the pretty Astrologer said to me, about really diving in deep to the exploration of this part of me, about the notion of taking on a lover. I will have to revisit how the Astrologer phrased it, but something about how it was to *nourish* me—to engage only with what feeds my Goddess within, the Queen that I am, as she phrased it. I know that I cannot be nourished by someone who is starving, themselves. What I desire is the company of a Seeker, like me; that we may explore together, grow together. That we may nourish one another.

So, there. We will see.

I am grateful that he shared with me his apprehensions about having the time and availability to "commit to a relationship in good faith that it would be fulfilling. I don't know where to go with that, currently," he texted. "Just giving you my honesty."

I do so deeply appreciate honesty.

So, perhaps a Friendship is what it will be for now, laced with attraction and desire. Perhaps this is the perfect distanced exploration for me right now, to go a little deeper into my own workings, and what that brings up for me—this beautiful Wolverine work of Art, this man. Let us see what this brings up for me.

Tuesday, December 1, 2020
3:00 a.m.

Here I am, awake since 2:00, mind whirring. Thinking about what it is that I desire, recognizing these curious patterns I fall into again and again. Fear. Loneliness. Longing. I think about where these feelings come from; what I learned by my mother leaving when I was three years old, though of course it was not her fault. And what I learned from my dad desperately missing her; his unfillable longing to mend the gaping wound that her displacement left. Is that what I learned? To spend a lifetime struggling with that same unquenchable desire? Yet pushing back against it, as well. A spiral of swirling loneliness, coupled with a fierce independence. The push-me-pull-you of my precarious steps, always seeking balance. Always a bit off, and wary.

I find myself thinking about when Bear and I were partners, how he was always there, always wonderfully ready to make himself available to me, to connect. It seemed that no sooner had young Fisher gone back to his dad's, Bear would be tapping at my front door. I loved that he was so into loving me, and also, I felt devoured sometimes, depleted by his appetite. Yet, when he took his attentions away from me, it was never long before I missed him terribly; missed that connection, that adoration, that support. When we parted ways the final time, sealed by him meeting the woman who is now his wife, I went through a substantial period of being awash with regret, of questioning having let him go. Yet I knew, at the same time, that it must be the true way for us. He and his new partner seemed like such a perfect fit for each other. With us, despite a solid friendship coupled with a primal ferocity to our love, something just never felt quite right.

So, here I am with a potential Love Interest waiting in the wings. Someone I am curious about, and attracted to, and also wary of, as seems prudent to be. Here I am kind of obsessing about him already, as seems to be my pattern with these sorts of things. I remind myself that even when Dan and I first began reconnecting a few weeks ago (is that all it was? Could it have been a couple of months ago?), I also began spinning in my little tizzies, based on romantic memories and residual feelings from our youth sparked in me, and not much more than that. Connection in curious little fits and starts with Dan, and red flags up the wazoo…marking the trail to where I am now, which is that it does not feel wise to encourage the exploration of our old friendship as anything other than that. I am grateful that he did not end up at my doorstep however many weeks ago, when he told me he was packing his bags and would be on his way soon. Initially I'd felt disappointed when he did not arrive as promised, but I reminded myself not to push the river (as Nana used to say), to just keep checking in with my heart and my internal guidance system, that whatever will be will be. To trust these angels watching over me, to know that they're doing a good job. To trust that they're protecting me, and have my best interest always at heart.

Now here I am with just this tiny taste of candy, in the flesh. The first man I have embraced in over a year who makes my little heart go pitter-pat, whose body calls out to mine. Late last summer on an impulsive trip to Wisconsin, I did not feel such a draw toward my newer friend, a Baker, though admittedly we'd both harbored some optimism of connecting in such a way. I very much enjoyed the ease of his company, but there was no energetic draw as lovers. Instead, I became enamored with the many acres of woods and fields around his hand-built home, with the smell of fresh bread baking in the brick oven, and the sounds of animals in the forest from where Anzu and I slept on the porch at night. I remember the Baker saying how I seemed more excited about his porch than by him, and, regrettably, his observation was true. It just was, there was nothing I could do about it. Oh, man, how I loved that porch.

On that trip, I did feel the draw of which I speak toward an old soul-brother lover-friend, which surely was unfortunate for me. The one day we were able to meet for a walk through a nature preserve, there was the old magnetic pull between our bodies as we embraced in the parking lot, as he gazed at me admiringly, he who has known me since back a quarter century. We walked hand-in-hand along the mown paths, through the intoxicating beauty of the Wisconsin landscape. Through trees and flowers and long grasses, pausing to admire butterflies, to take pictures, to speak as old friends about what we are learning in life. So strong was the energy between us, the pull of my long-time Piscean soul-friend. When his gentle goodbye kiss lingered, it melted into the impassioned kiss of a lover, of Love. As my breath quickened at the taste of his tongue, my heartbeat emboldened by the sweetness of his lips, by an old familiarity to his breath, and then—

No.
There was this:

He was not for me to keep, my old friend. He had promised himself to another. Though this momentary delusion suggested otherwise, he was not available to offer himself to me. And that, most certainly, was NOT what I need.

Halfway back to Colorado, I spoke on the phone of this kiss to my best bestie, Brandi, who did not understand why I was crying. I could not explain to her the aching in my chest, because I also did not understand.

And now—what of Beorn?
A curiosity.
Is he available to offer himself to me?
Is he available to reveal himself as truly *what I need?*

* * * * * *

I would like to interject here from modern-day times, that—spoiler alert—Beorn does NOT turn out to be the man of my dreams. The man of fantasies, most certainly, and at times, eventually, a good friend. But not the man of my overarching *dreams.* This is not going to be a Love Story about Beorn, or any other man, for that matter. It is, in fact, a Love Story about me, myself. About finding a path to falling in love with all my complicated, complex, multi-faceted (and often messy) workings, in ways that have long felt elusive, at best. I mean really, and for Real. As the saying goes, you will never be able to truly love someone else until you first truly love yourself. I know this to be accurate. On the deepest levels, in the most hidden and sneakiest of ways, when you are finally able to love your Self—I mean, REALLY LOVE YOUR SELF—that's the *only* path toward experiencing and expressing such love for others, in purest form.

I mean *really*, and for Real.

So, if you had your heart set on a story where the handsome hero becomes the solution for all that ails a girl, now would be a good time to abandon this version of a Fairy Tale. Or you could hang in there a while longer (with a little optimism, thank you), and see how this version goes.

I have considered a great deal just how much of the Beorn parts I wish to include in this story, because in my journals he's going to keep coming up quite a lot for a while, and then some. To be honest, it's a little embarrassing how much I distracted myself with him, and also, that was so much a part of what I needed yet to learn.

As of this writing, Beorn and I still communicate from time to time, and he still gives me a run for my money, emotionally and otherwise. In talking this over with Brandi yesterday, the point I made to her was that I recognize this story is not at all about him, and still, he became such a powerful facilitator for bits and pieces of what I had to learn. He became a fabulous, excruciating trigger for me, for my imbedded patterns and deeply buried issues, from long, long before he and I became involved. A trigger for all that I needed unearthed and held painfully in front of my face, as I engaged in the most intensive Self Work of my life as I know it yet. Beorn became my trigger, my mirror, my father-figure, confidante, lover, and nemesis, all bundled into one—whether he was up for it or not. Dare say, the poor fellow was not up for it at all, awash in his own many things ("I don't *want* to be your trigger," he protested more than once). All the same, to this day, I am grateful for his role in the many insights gleaned, in helping to illuminate what was difficult for me to see. The Reluctant Hero, as one might call him, eventually revealing himself to be exactly and perfectly (in the grander scheme of things) both what I did, and what I did not really need.

* * * * * *

It seems as though Beorn desires my admiration and validation, just as I have felt from him in brief interactions in our past, and what I've witnessed of his behavior from afar. So, yes, now close up, it is no surprise that's what I'm noticing. I enjoy the attention of it directed toward me; this seeking of approval so far as to finally ask me outright (by Messenger, not to my face, mind you) if I am attracted to him, to which I felt hesitant to answer, albeit truthfully: Yes, indeed I am.

Now there is silence from him again.

It reminds me of an experience with a fellow years ago, who turned out to be a perfect broken-winged bird for me, missing arm and all. The way he gushed over me for that first weekend after we'd met at a talk he was giving, then confessed after leaving town that he wasn't in a place for a Relationship, but would like to see me again…And I didn't really listen, I suppose, I heard what I wanted to hear. I reached out to him regularly, offering my support regarding some stressful Life Challenges he was dealing with. I suppose part of me thought he would feel endeared by my caring and availability, but of course it had the opposite effect. I ended up becoming "needy" in his eyes, though I bristled at this eventual remark. Admittedly, *needy* was exactly how I felt—desperate for the attention he had lavished upon me in the beginning. Desperate for the drug that tasted like love.

(That is not what real love tastes like, my dear.)

I do not want what some seem to offer me; the chaos, confusion, and strife. What I wish for, what my heart truly desires, is health, balance, reciprocity...Real love. Not just some freakin' drug.

When Beorn and I were walking up the woodland slope, we spoke of social media, of dopamine releases, and addictions. He asked if I have any addictions that I struggle with, and I laughed, hesitating only momentarily before blurting out, "Well, the first things that come to mind are cute boys, and chocolate."

He paused, looked at me. I laughed nervously. I had to explain what I meant, which lead to a conversation most delicious to my palate...conversation which felt like Real Talk to me. We seemed to both be coming from a place of honest vulnerability as we spoke of our challenges in past relationships, and of being "too much" for some.

"But for other people," I added, "I am just the right amount."

For some people, it seems this is exactly what they appreciate about me—my forthrightness, my authenticity. For me, it was so sexy to get to the meat of these issues in our first real interaction, even in the brief amount of time he'd been able to carve out of his busy schedule for a conversation in the flesh. It was vastly alluring to me that when he'd overstayed his allotted time by forty-five minutes, I felt we had much more we could talk about, and I did not want him to leave. So lovely that I wanted to keep touching him. To grab his strong arms, to hook my heel around his leg, and try, laughing, to get him down to the snowy ground. I was like a child trying to wrestle down a tree.

In reply to my later confession, he texted, "You want me on the ground? All you have to do is ask. Want me on my knees? Just ask."

Oooooh, boy.

It is so easy for me to get lost in what feels like true connection, to get swept away in what I wish to be Real. My desire is not only for the physical connective magic, but for all the intense creative energy it brings. I want to touch, to feel, to taste, to express that Love (or is it lust?). That desire becomes my drug.

And I can become insatiable.

That's a good thing for me to look at.

Wednesday, December 2, 2020
3:35 a.m.

"What we resist persists," I was told in *Conversations with God,* by Neale Donald Walsch. What did God say next? That what we look at disappears? Something like that. I'm not sure what that means, exactly, but here I am. Looking.

So, there is this Fear thing for me.
There is this fucking loneliness.
There is this insecurity, this doubting my own value, my own worth.

All of it—ALL of it—is coming up twenty-fold. I draw these demons to myself most effectively through the forms of beautiful (dangerous) men; visibly strong and promising depth, but ultimately unavailable emotionally. This is no coincidence, what with my complicated relationship with the first man in my life, who as a little girl was nothing short of God to me. Father: the one who I feared, and also longed deeply to be seen by. To have his approval, his affection, to have value in his eyes. This is where it all gets a little jumbled for me in terms of what I think I am doing, what I'm trying to sort out around these issues by drawing these men to me.

I'm having a flashback to a walk by the river with Dad a few years ago, when I was struggling with scary drama around a fellow I'd been involved with on and off for more than a year. A fellow who I'd had reservations about over many years of being friendly acquaintances, but (after a painful breakup, and feeling very lonely) got drawn in by his charming words and ways, doing all the right things to convince me he was a good friend. When we became involved more intimately, the shiny surface illusions gave way to deeper darknesses, which I somehow thought I could help mend—the broken-winged bird thing, which comes up for me again and again. Especially when I ended things, he continued reaching out to me, insistently. As my dad and I walked along the river, the guy was texting me angrily, as had become part of his pattern. Sometimes he'd call me at all hours of the night to spew drunken, toxic venom through the phone at me, to tell me how awful I was. Rather than just turning off my phone, I'd try to pacify him, to help him through his rage and pain. He always apologized profusely within days, telling me how special and important I was to him. A couple of times he showed up swaying toward my doorstep, and I'd instinctively try to make out if he had a gun. Fisher knew that if the guy ever showed up in such a manner to go inside immediately and be ready to dial 911.

I confessed to my dad a bit of this mess I'd become entangled in, as I'm sure I must have been visibly shaken. I remember Dad saying to me in a tone which rang accusatory to my ears, "DON'T YOU LOVE YOURSELF ENOUGH NOT TO ALLOW SOMEONE LIKE THAT IN YOUR LIFE?"

The intensity of his words stung, driven deeply home. At the time, I don't believe that I *did* know how to love myself enough, apparently, otherwise why would I allow myself to suffer such verbal and emotional abuse? Some part of me felt that not only could I handle the drama, but that I somehow deserved it, too. Some part of it felt comfortable to me, even craving it, as messed up as that sounds. Of course, I thought I could fix the guy; I could understand and help him in a way no other woman could. I'm guessing this is pretty classic textbook disfunction, here, that I believed, by saving this guy from his chaos, his brokenness, his toxicity and his pain, I would be saved, myself. That by liberating the light I saw flickering way down deep inside of him, I would become worthy of Love.

The best thing to come from the conversation with my dad was that I was broken enough to open to the parts of him that were kind, and caring, and generous. Those parts of Dad who wanted nothing more than to love, and to be loved. The parts of him that wanted to Help. On that day by the river, I cried in his presence. I confessed I didn't know what to do. He asked if I ever thought of going to the Hoffman Process, a week-long, guided self-exploration retreat in California, which had been profoundly life-altering for him twenty-some years earlier. I remember it was like he came back a different man; more loving and open, not angry and stern as I had mostly known him. I told him that, yes, I had long been curious about the Process and would be willing to give it a try, but that the cost and logistics of such an excursion had always seemed too formidable. He told me plainly that he would help me figure it out, for whatever I needed to make it happen. I paused, silently considering this proposition which felt uncomfortably new to me after what seemed like a lifetime of being responsible for meeting my own needs. That he was offering, and that I could let him help me. I took a deep breath, and said, "Thank you."

That was a huge moment for my dad and me. One I can look back on with gratitude.

Indeed, the Hoffman Process ended up facilitating a huge shift for me. Another of those times when the doors of perception opened further, where my insights and perspectives widened dramatically. It also became a precursor for many more insights that were soon to come. It was the first tremors of what would grow into earth-shattering, tectonic plate-moving shifts for me.

So, here's the thing, and it's important to keep reminding myself, lest I allow myself to slide down the muddy slope toward old, unhelpful patterns again, toward these broken-winged birds of men. I _do love myself_ more than to allow disfunction and abuse into my world, not to mention the worlds of my beloved child, and my animal family. I _do_ have respect for myself, and I honor my own needs. I can have compassion for and be of assistance to others, while still maintaining healthy boundaries and taking care of Me.

This is the part that feels exciting in its newness to me, in its harvesting of resilience and strength. These notions are what I wish to continue cultivating, they are what feel helpful to me. The re-programming of some old, worn-out patterns, of that which no longer serves me. The knowing that health and balance are available to me, if I can only figure out how to get there. Also, the honoring of where others are on their own given paths, the place where they (wittingly or not so much) have chosen for themselves to be. To not get roped into that which does not serve me, ultimately. To follow the wisdom that I am earning. To keep learning.

Sweet Mother, I am making progress, at last.

"Great, kid! Don't get cocky on me."

— Han Solo

Something I noticed on my Sunday walk with Beorn is that he doesn't really ask me questions, but he's pretty good at talking about himself. I believe this is common, and I get it, I've been there, too. It's easy to become self-occupied, especially when feeling nervous or vulnerable, and when desiring the approval of another. At one point I thought to myself, "Stop asking questions, now, Laura. Stop talking. Let him ask some questions now, let him reach out to me. Or let there just be silence."

That is where I am again now, and it feels like a good place to be.
Let it breathe, let it breathe, let it be.

Sunday, December 6, 2020
4:40 a.m.

I will not be wooed by chiseled abs and pectoral muscles like slabs of stone. I will not be wooed by strong arms and rugged hands, by an intense look (in a photograph) in his eyes. I will not be wooed by that muscle—you know the one—the muscle that extends near the hip, down along the lower side of a man's abdomen, to his groin…the one that I want to caress, to kiss…I will not be wooed by that.

Give me some communication to go along with all that sexiness. Give me some depth, and true connection. If there is not time (or desire) for that from his end, then the entire endeavor will not be worth my while. And Life is too precious for that.

I am grateful for the opportunity to explore these notions, to find clarity. Whatever the outcome ends up being with the handsome Beorn, I will continue to feel grateful for this.

Good.
Thank you.

Ashaya comes trotting downstairs from my bedroom, where she and Anzu have been sleeping while I write down here in the guest room. She is happy to see me, in her tiny prancing pony-dog display, and tells me excitedly that she would like to go outside, please—for *that*, I am grateful, too. That means no poop or pee in the house, by golly, which has been a blessing long and hard won. These tiny blessings fill me with such gratitude, like the tiny, trembling, huge-eared pixie creature, telling me she needs to go out.

7:57 p.m.

Askew.

Maybe I'm thinking too much, always processing so many thoughts in my mind. Do I really need to process so much, all the time? Do I really need all of these words?

Listening to Jay Shetty's book this morning while I did yoga, that was my multi-tasking. He spoke of how multi-tasking is one of those monkey-mind things, and, yep, that's exactly what I was doing. All of this writing, I don't even know why…it's like I'm trying to write myself to some place of solace, to write away all of this loneliness. If I had someone to share all my thoughts with, would I still keep writing? Would it still be such a compulsion? Or would my loneliness be squelched, my obsessive desire for expression fulfilled? Would all of my questions be answered, finally, or would I just not feel the need to ask them anymore?

This morning I went to work-out at a girlfriend's "porch gym," as she calls it. She put me on the elliptical in the garage for a mere ten minutes, and despite breaking into a good sweat, I kept thinking, *THIS IS BORING AS FUCK*. Where am I going? Nowhere—that's where. Nowhere in this garage, that's for darned sure. I was just cranky, not really sure what my problem was. Even just chatting with my friend and her partner, I found myself cursing a whole lot.

Maybe I'm just not comfortable here. Maybe I'm just not comfortable in my own skin.

I feel askew.

After Porch Gym, I drove the dogs over to the baseball field and attempted to take them for a walk along the river. I got not quite as far as one of the small lakes along the treed pathway—ten minutes or so—then got freaked out hearing a dog barking from one of the condos and couldn't see what was around the bend. So we turned around and walked quickly back to the truck, with grumbling in my brain.

I keep thinking: *I DON'T KNOW WHAT I FUCKING WANT.*

I feel as though I am teetering on the edge of some dream. Who is in this dream? What the fuck is happening? How the fuck did I get here, and what the fuck is going to happen next? We humans and our desire to understand and control everything, all the time.

I JUST DON'T WANT TO BE SCARED OF EVERYTHING ALL THE TIME ANYMORE.

I want to know why I am fucking scared all the time. What a crazy waste of life.

I feel like Basquiat, or what I have learned of Basquiat, at the point where his complexion was all a mess and he didn't seem to know which way to turn. Yet, here I am, my life is pretty simple—two dogs snoring by my side. Still, when fresh off the phone from a conversation with an old, dear girlfriend, there it was waiting for me—that bone-crushing loneliness, the pain in my heart and chest which makes me feel like reeling, like collapsing to the ground.

It confuses me—*What the Fuck Is This???* Where does this come from? What on Earth am I supposed to *do* with *THIS?*

I can do all the house chores, I can clean the aquarium filters, I can vacuum the carpet, I can move the geranium plant hither and yon (that part was my favorite, the way it smelled as it brushed against my skin). I can watch that movie, *Basquiat*, again. I can feed the dogs and take them for a walk outside in the cool night air, silently, in the dark. As Anzu awakens on the bed now, she looks at me and sighs, and I can feel pressingly in my heart the weight of how much I love her. I can do and feel all of these things, and still, there is something missing—some grand and urgent mystery—something that keeps me ensnared in my own fear and aching loneliness, my pain. There is something out there, or something in here…there is something that I need to look at, to illuminate, to learn how not to resist. There is something in me that needs to be healed. I think there's something I need to know, and then learn how to let it go.

"The *intention* underlying every action is what causes
it to resonate with a lower or higher frequency.
You have lived many lifetimes unaware that you were
powerful beings, creators, embodying all the qualities
of Source.
But you know it now, and at some point, must actually
accept it."

— Arcturian Group Message, December 2020

I need to let it go.

Wednesday, December 9, 2020
around 4:00 a.m.

There is this compulsion I have to write all of these thoughts down, to expunge them from my mind, even though there are so many more than I can ever capture. The continual motion of images and ideas like laundry in a dryer, colors and textures keep tumbling, but it is difficult to sort them out…I need to stop the dryer. Take the articles of clothing out one piece at a time, fold them neatly, put them where they go. It is no coincidence that at this moment I have a dryer-load of clothes that have been in there for several days, waiting patiently to be folded and put away. There is another pile of dirty clothes waiting to be washed, but first I need to clear out the drier…dirty clothes pile metaphors abound.

Thursday, December 10, 2020
7:32 a.m.

I am still in the thick of something emotionally, that's for sure. When I came inside from taking the dogs for a pee, I felt a hot flash and a wave of emotion that I couldn't quite put my finger on. As I got to the stove to check on my gruel (from my Baker friend with the glorious country home in Wisconsin), I began to cry.

I miss my home in the country. I miss having a big, fenced-in yard. I miss my horse, and my llama. I miss the trees, the birds, and the deer.

Then there is all the emotion and vulnerability I had laid out on the table moments earlier, by way of a wordy message to Beorn. There are all the feelings of necessity in doing so, coupled with all of the fear…

Fear of what, pray tell, my darling?

Fear of not being understood, not being valued, not being seen.

Then, in my mind, through my pen, the soothing voice comes to me:

The only way that someone might see you, my dear, is to show yourself to them. This is why you wear your heart on your sleeve—it is your offering to the World. Some may know just what to do with that—they may respect you for your integrity, and know how to reciprocate. Others may not understand, it could even be frightening for them, and may send them to a hasty retreat. That is fine, my darling, that is really about Them, not a reflection of who You are and what value you hold. Stay true your course. Stay your honesty, your integrity. You put out there some good Truths today. You are releasing expectations of reciprocity, while still holding out a space for it to be received, should he be willing, and capable, and desirous of that, as well. You are staying open, and that will serve you, dear. Come from Love, and stay open to the flow.

Take care of yourself, my darling, my sweet.

You are so very loved.

Chapter 6
Letting Go

"We think that the point is to pass the test or overcome the problem, but the truth is that things don't really get solved. They come together and they fall apart. Then they come together again and fall apart again. It's just like that. The healing comes from letting there be room for all of this to happen: room for grief, for relief, for misery, for joy."

— Pema Chödrön

I will interject again here that the writing of this book has gotten to a difficult point for me. Even a couple of days ago I was super revved-up about it, feeling that all was going so smoothly, that really this endeavor of mine is turning out to be a piece of cake. Granted, this is after putting the project aside for several months, though thinking about it regularly, always in the back of my mind. When I got the Covid recently, presumably at an intimate Michael Franti concert, which was outdoors and so very lovely, and also, a total dancing, sweating, laughing, hugging-strangers love-fest. So, worth the getting sick, one might say, but it completely knocked me on my ass. As in, all I could do was sleep, cough, and ache, and toss and turn miserably for days. While I was in that haze, and for a good couple of weeks afterward, it felt very much as though I had been on a Medicine Journey, like coming out the other side of a Spiritual quest…and knowing it was time to begin writing this book again.

If you've not seen the movie *Scott Pilgrim vs. the World* you really must, if for no other reason (though there are plenty) than you will understand the voice in my head of Scott Pilgrim whining, "*...but it's haaaarrrd!!*" That is the voice I was hearing all yesterday afternoon, and well into the evening, as I scrutinized the journal I've been scrutinizing, trying to find the bits and pieces which feel appropriate, fitting, and important for this book. Fer cryin' in the milk, I mean, *geeze*—I am five chapters in and haven't even gotten through December of 2020. I haven't even gotten to where...well, where things get *super* hard. I mean, where I start to crash and burn, and question reality and everything. I haven't even gotten to the part where Dan dies.

It's hard—really hard—to read about after having not opened those journal pages since I wrote on them. It's hard to experience all those feelings again, through my words. It's hard not to get drawn back into that loneliness, and pain.

So maybe that's exactly what I'm supposed to do with it again. Maybe the *allowing* for those sensations, the process of *really feeling them* and *letting them in*—maybe that is exactly what I've been getting at all this time; it is the dance of three steps forward and two steps back, then three steps forward again.

I reached out to Beorn last night, from the depths of my loneliness and despair. "Why so lonely?" he texted back. I told him about the journals I've been pouring through, how much emotion it's bringing up. He told me he'd burned his old journals because they were more sadness than he needed to hold on to, as he phrased it. I can understand that fully, and, as I replied, "Mine are also full of redemption, gratitude, learning, and growth. Especially over the past two years. I need to skip ahead to those parts. I'm getting bogged down in the painful parts, before I began the Journey Work."

So, yes. And also...There are some pieces which feel important for me to include, even if only for sentimental reasons. Life feels hard sometimes, and as for this book, I guess I never really thought it would be easy. Not all the way through it, at any rate—just like Life. Sometimes it's easy and feels like a dream. Sometimes it can feel like a freakin' nightmare. You just keep on plugging through, or you'll miss all the bits of it.

Three steps forward, two steps back. Three steps forward again.

* * * * * *

Sunday, December 13, 2020

I puttered around the house a lot this morning, listening to the book *The Untethered Soul* by Michael Singer through Dad's old stereo system. Got a couple of projects done, spun in some circles, too. I found myself on the landing amid the staircase, having plucked a couple of old journals from the bookshelf. I sat on the carpet, reading them there. Journals from the days of living in Wisconsin on the goat farm, long before my Colorado life. I found a note from the summer of my New York City love coming to live with me while his band was on a break from touring. In his handwriting, the small square of paper read, "I am having a good time! More kisses, please!" I could almost hear his joyous laughter.

I read an entry about lying in bed with the dreamy friend who stepped in after my summer love left, sealing that uncertain future's fate. About how I couldn't tell this friend (whom I'd admired for many years) what I was thinking when he asked me. I was unable to share with him, laying there, how profoundly, terrifyingly beautiful he was to me.

I read about being in the basement recording studio of my Midwestern muse, the one I wrote of as a butterfly—how we were listening to the Elliot Smith CD, "XO," we'd just bought at B-Side Records in Madison, on State Street. It was then he confessed that when he'd read my writing entitled "Good Friday" (which I'd tucked for him into the front pages of the book, *Conversations with God*), he realized he was in love with me.

Reading all these words made me cry, sitting on that landing amid my staircase—*oh, my heart, my heart!* So much beauty, so much passion, and so much pain. So much exquisite love I have known in short bursts. So much poetry, and grace.

I was nearly in tears at the grocery store this afternoon, after a masked-up friend punched me playfully on the arm, and I returned his gesture with a toothy grin obscured by my own mask. I felt desperate for that physical connection.

Tonight, I just felt wretched, sobbing to myself. Against my better judgement, I texted something to Beorn about "My Kingdom for a bubble bath built for two." How vulnerable I felt even sending those words. But lo and behold, he replied with three little hearts, and words saying, "I can come see you tomorrow?"

Not a question, more a declaration, it seemed.

And I burst into tears again, I cried and cried by the kitchen counter. "Yes, please," I replied.

(He never did arrive.)

Tuesday, December 15, 2020
5:44 a.m.

I was struck by an interview on the Rich Roll Podcast yesterday with an Olympic swimmer named Caroline. The discussion was of trauma, and how it manifests in the body, can even be passed along genetically, and how it creates obstacles on the path of (in essence) letting our true lights shine. This all plays into the resonating themes in my life, in my thoughts, about how we create our own realities, and what that ends up looking like for us as individuals, as well as for Humanity as a collective whole. I think about this so often; about what I am creating. It is a theme which has come up for me again and again and again over many years. The theme of how I process Trauma, which has been boldly in my face for the past couple of years, since Aspen the Great Pyrenees had that good nibble on my legs—releasing so many demons I hadn't realized were hiding deep inside of me. "New trauma triggers old trauma," as a counselor later professed to me. Releasing so many fears and insecurities I'd been pushing down for years, but which always have their subconscious play on how I walk through life. I suppose I should be grateful to that big, toothy white dog who sent me to the ER to get torn skin stitched, to get punctures flushed and sanitized. I should be grateful for the scars now on my legs and in my muscle tissue, the ones that scream to me every time I'm around a new dog. I should be thankful to have this discomfort put so boldly in my face that I cannot turn away from it in good conscience. The trauma rises to teach me some things—to remind me of some things—about who I really am.

So, who am I, really?
I mean, REALLY?

This morning since shortly after getting up, I've had the Alanis Morrisette song "All I Really Want" in my head. It feels so much to the point of where I am right now. All these visions I have of a home in the country, of the Partner to build it with me. Visions, sensations of the animals both wild and domestic, of the gardens, of the greenery, and nurturing space all around. The space for our family, our friends, our loves. I see myself continuing on my path of learning, and growth; continuing to write, and to share. I feel the support, the security, the healing energy there. I can feel it in my heart, this vision that I see. I can *feel* it.

Remember this feeling.

This is helping me to hone my vision, these sensations. This is helping me find my own wisdom, and magic. This is helping me to set my intentions, and open to the possibilities. To let go and allow all of this to flow. To allow me to welcome unequivocally into my truth, of *who I choose to be.*

I hear my beautiful child stir in his bed in the room above my head. Let the fears and apprehensions visit me, if they will. I will touch them like a feather to bubbles; I will acknowledge them and let them go. I will feel and see and hear the encouragement around me. All signs point to fulfillment of the dream I have long been having, of it taking form in this three-dimensional realm. The time has never been better to plant these seeds and nurture them, to allow them to grow. Allow this vision to flow. Trust, and trust, and trust. Allow this vision to grow.

Wednesday December 30, 2020
7:14 a.m.

Full moon setting over the mountains in a lavender sky— the very shade, I swear it, that I envisioned in the flows of an Abundance Meditation I was listening to half an hour ago, the one I opened my eyes from, feeling enlivened, inspired, invigorated. Feeling optimistic in a way I had not felt for several days. My God, the sky is so beautiful now as the full, round moon dips closer to the snowy peaks; as they begin to reflect the softest shades of pinky-orange from the other end of the sky.

I was asking Fisher yesterday, as we drove home discussing what we appreciate about our townhouse, what we should choose to recreate in a home that we built ourselves...I told him I will love to have windows all around the house (pointedly absent from our townhome, due to the Siamese twin nature of such structures), because I do so love to watch the rising sun, and the moon as it travels across the night sky. I love to wake up to its cool and soothing presence in the darkness, an ethereal friend who has been watching over me like a child where I sleep and dream, assuring that I am safe.

(Dear child, sleep, and know that you are Safe.)

I can feel that peace inside of me.

Again, I will express—I am so grateful for our home right now. I am grateful for the comfort and luxury of this place which was my father's, he with his impeccable taste. I am grateful for the protecting, guiding elements of the presence of my dad, which I feel lingering here (sometimes mischievously) as we ready ourselves to continue stepping forward into the next versions of our dreams—to decide and then to act upon what we chose those visions to be. This is our warm and loving pausing point. This is the place to get our bearings and gain insights, before stepping forward once again with balance and powerful grace. This is the gentle flow of the moment—this moment—to reflect upon all that I've learned and am learning, all these insights and epiphanies and creative power that is building in my chest, building in the ether around me. These visions become clearer, of *who I choose to be.*

My greatest challenge, historically, has been getting clear on what I *want.* I remember Nana lamenting to me in my late twenties about my seeming lack of a future/family/career path, "Honey, you're good at so many things—you just have to *pick one.*" It has often been my stumbling block, perhaps my reason to proceed through life so gingerly. At a snail's pace, some might say.

The Universe is patient with me, and will wait.

What do you choose to call forth, dear one?
What do you truly choose to create?
In your heart of hearts, what visions do you hold?
What do you truly BELIEVE?

You Create What You Truly Believe.

Remember this, always. Remember it, again and again. Now, my darling, my precious one,

CHOOSE what you will believe.

Thoughts + words + action = CREATION, as we choose our own reality.

Thursday, December 31, 2020
Sometime after 5 a.m.

Coffee and goat milk, cat loaf purring at my feet.

Today is the last day of 2020, and I'm sure there will be many who will say, *Good Riddance!* Beorn said to me yesterday (standing outside the library, while still in my embrace) that "this will be the best new year yet!" I added that the next one will be even better, and the one after that will be better still! At least, that is certainly what I can hope for myself, and for anyone else, if they so wish. That things can just keep getting better and better from this point forward. It is only a question of how we go about creating this, that's what I want to know. That's what I am striving for. That's what I am listening and watching for, as often as I can. One moment at a time. One footstep in front of the other.

I met up with Beorn on the street outside the library yesterday, for only a few minutes, we'd agreed, as he was heading to work to blow up avalanches and I was heading out to clean horse stalls at the barn. I felt so grateful to finally see him again in the flesh, as I had not since our first nature walk five weeks earlier, with only erratic communication since then. It seems funny, and surreal, like some dream of a man I'm curious about, but who is mostly composed of ideas I've come up with in my own mind, fueled by images and words he's sent me directly, with blanks filled in by other images and poetic rants he's posted on Facebook. Then there he was—see, I didn't make him up!—walking toward me on the snowy street, all baseball cap and sunglasses and dirty Carhartt's of a working man (so hot), with his Melanzana hoodie over strong shoulders, torso, and arms. He lifted me easily from the ground (no small feat at my Covid bonus size), and I laughed, wrapping my legs and clunky muck boots all baby-monkey style around his slender waist. He held me gently like an old, familiar lover, or maybe like some long-lost friend. He held me in the sweetest embrace, right there by our small-town park, for God and everyone to see. Oh, to breathe that manly sweetness of his neck, of his curly hair—he smelled amazing, like wood. I told him so, with arms wrapped firmly around his shoulders, my chin tucked into the crook of his neck.

"I always smell like wood," was his reply, muffled into my scarf.

Oh, to kiss his bearded cheek, the handsome silver peppering of his face—only distantly wondering at photos he'd sent, that he said he'd taken the week before, though I felt sure that in them his beard was fully black. I do not know the mysteries of this man, I only know that my body comes aglow at his touch, at the feel of his strong hands. At the joy in hearing him say that *Now He Does Not Want to Go to Work.* To breathe him in as our faces turn toward one another, our lips meeting in the most gentle, lingering kiss. Oh, such bliss, to feel his beard against my chin.

This is a Grand Beginning, I thought to myself, holding on firmly to him.

A grand potential for what may be explored on down the road.

In that moment, it was perfect, and beautiful, and magically surreal. If there is more of that to be relished and explored, well, I will have it, please—I will welcome more.

I let loose my grip, slid back to the ground. Reluctantly, he let me go. With both of us beaming toothy grins and wishes for a Happy New Year, we parted ways as the sun set slowly in the west.

January 2, 2021
6:15 a.m.

This morning I came down the carpeted stairs from our bedrooms, in the dark, cradling two drinking jars in my arms. I was thinking about the idea of being a Spirit in a body versus being a body with a Spirit. I'd been reading about that again last night in *Conversations with God, Book 4,* and remembering Rich Roll saying in one of his interviews that when he first got into rehab, someone asked which he believed he was. At the time he'd replied, "I don't even know what that *MEANS*...."

As I pondered that notion, I really felt it in my body—the feeling of truly being a Spirit *within* a body, for the soul purpose of having this experience we call Life. In the dark, I took what

I thought was the last step to the landing, instead finding my foot falling upon air. Down I went, landing hard on the floor, with my legs crumpled awkwardly beneath me, with my elbows bracing my fall. Amazingly, the jars I held did not break, staying securely within my grasp. Curiously, I'd heard myself laugh as I went down; I felt no startling or fear. As I gathered myself easily to rise from the floor, I mused at how the landing had not hurt me one bit. It was funny. With that idea of being truly Spirit inhabiting a body, it was as though my spirit decided to take my body for a brief flight—airborne for that moment. Free.

Oh, my, I thought. *To carry such liberation into every moment of every day. What a glorious blessing that would be.*

Tuesday, January 5, 2021
7:33 a.m.

The mountains seem to be obscured by a magical mist this morning, a veil of purples and pinks and blues. The morning sunlight stretches out across the valley to lay golden upon the evergreens at the mountains' base, and the patches of white snow amongst the clusters of trees.

It is difficult for me to write about this, about so many feelings swirling around like bats from a cave, like some tempest of emotion. I shared some thoughts in a Facebook post in his honor yesterday morning, accompanied by an old blurry photograph of me and Dan at his apartment in Madison when I visited over Christmas while home from Arizona (so must have been early '90s). He had one arm around my waist, the other akimbo, with fist perched at his hip, his blurry face turned toward me, beaming. What a curious (and caring) friendship we always had.

When I received the message Saturday morning from the girlfriend I didn't know Dan had, I had the same sort of moment I remember fifteen years ago, of my world spinning as I looked at the plus symbol on a pregnancy test, a distinct sense of reality shifting all around me. Part of me could not believe that it could be true. A deeper part of me knew that it was. Dan was dead. My friend was gone. Could this really be? But he just texted me the day before New Year's. He just told me he missed me, and that he would see me soon.

I messaged his girlfriend back immediately, asking if she would please call me. When she told me the news again over the phone, my first words of acknowledgment were "Mother-fucker—" and I began to cry. I may not have been completely surprised by the news, but my sense of heartbreak was complete.

Mother-fucker.
So, this is what he chose, after all.
Oh, boy, these are some uncomfortable feelings.

Stop eating, now, Laura, you are full.
Step outside into the light of the rising sun.
Good job.
Now, write.

Dan's girlfriend and I spoke on the phone yesterday morning for what felt like a couple of hours.

There is a lot of information for me to unpack, and this morning is not the time in which I wish to commit to that work. This morning, what I wish is to continue attending to my own needs, and to the needs of these beloved creatures. I have dog clients waiting alone at their home while their human parents are still at the hospital in Colorado Springs, praying for their infant daughter's life.

There is so much in Life; so much to choose, so much to move forward with.

Bottom line is, Dan left his body. He will not be coming from Madison to visit me. He will no longer be texting me or calling me on the phone. All of that is over, settled once and for all. He is released from the body that was breaking down on him, after so many years of misuse and neglect. If a grand shift had been on the horizon for him, this is it. It is done.

His girlfriend texted yesterday after our conversation, saying the autopsy results were "unclear."

"He did have substantial coronary artery blockage, but not definitive," she wrote. "Tox screen results may not be available for several months. Jesus."

So, no facts to wrap our monkey brains around, no conclusive explanations to help us make sense of this or that. Maybe it was a heart attack. Maybe it was a drug overdose. We won't know for some time…which is fine. The take-away for me is the same, either way:

> Life is precious.
> Our bodies are our temples.
> Love.
> Learn.
> Breathe.
> Smile.
> Drink lots of water.
> Keep on doing Good Things.
> Keep on being a Good Person.
> Let go when it's time to.
> Move on.

Thank you, Dan. I love you.

> "You catch what you're close to."
> — Reverend Steven Furtick,
> Regarding those with whom we choose to align.

Wednesday, January 6, 2021
5:13 a.m.

When the feeling crept into me gently on the evening of New Year's day, I walked from Ryan's art studio, having exchanged I love you's with Fisher, and kissed the little dog, Manu, goodbye—I knew it would not stay. The feeling. Not forever, not always. I knew that the feeling would come and go, as it always must. I was just grateful when it sat beside me on the sofa, hunkered in with smiles and contentment alongside the dogs and cat and myself as we watched a movie which ended well. I was grateful to feel it wrapped around me when I climbed into bed, tiny dog cradled in my arms at my chest, big dog pressed to the tops of my legs, and a smile lit gently on my sleepy face. The feeling kissed me sweetly, fed me beautiful dreams through the night. It was there when I yawned and stretched in the morning...I wondered if it might actually stay with me forever, this feeling. I wondered if it was my new reality.

But, no, not forever, not always, my dear. That is not the way of these things. You may as well wish for the sun to hang always in the sky, to never feel the dark kiss of night. You may as well try to halt the ebb and flow of the tides.

Chapter 7
The Keepers

"How easily I can hold space for difficulty, but really, I know
I'm called to be a keeper of joy.
The kind of joy that's harvested from midnight gardens.
The kind of joy that's cut into the night sky so light can leak
through. Unyielding, impenetrable starlight.
A keeper of joy. Like you."

— Laura Thomas

Friday, January 8, 2021
Probably around 5 a.m.

This whole Beorn thing. I am not feeling very patient about
it anymore. I am chomping at the bit. A kiss over a week ago (in
times of Pandemic, no less) kept me satiated for a day or two,
then I found myself reaching out, wanting more...words, images,
sentiments, ideas. His replies are a trickle, at best. I have been
in this position several times in my life, intrigued by a soul—
wanting to touch, to taste, to know—and the wanting does not
feel reciprocal, it only serves to push them away. So, knowing
what I know, and (hopefully) learning what I have learned of
this tendency in myself—to choose the ones who are beautiful,

mysterious, and **elusive**—what do I now choose to do with what I have learned? How do I choose to next engage, or to disengage, with the scenario at hand?

(This is not what I need.)

It has always been a challenge for me, to let these elusive butterflies leave; to stop chasing them, stop pining for them, stop longing for them to be near. Oh, boy, you can look at my entire dating history, beginning with the colorful Rolando, a' way up in Minnesota. Oh, how I longed for him, as he came and went from my town. Oh, how that boy stoked the fires of my heart when I was all of sixteen years old. With his fingernails painted black, the smell of oil paints in his clothes, singing love songs by The Cure to me, dancing around me all jingle-jangle, seductively... but ultimately unavailable, in the long run.

Here we are thirty-some years on down the road, and is it me still creating this perfect scenario? Nowadays, that looks like a strong, rugged, bearded man, who's building his own house by milling logs with a freaking chainsaw, fer cryin' out loud. Who drives a big, beefy truck which (weirdly) makes my nether regions tingle. Who has no fear of avalanches (nor any other physical thing, it would seem) and a sincere look in his eye. Whom I hear speak sweetly to his daughter over the phone. Who says he's into canning, and reading books. Who wears dirty Carhartts and smells like wood. Who quotes poetry on his freakin' Facebook page by the likes of Frida Kahlo. Who doles out just enough endearment to make me wonder, to make me long for more.

Yes. Perfect.

He is my dream, apparently—the one I have created this time. The one who fulfills this part of me who is terrified of getting too close, because she knows they will always leave her. She holds the banner above my head (the one the psychic saw in my early twenties) with steadfast certainty, lest I forget. The banner declaring: "LOVE = LOSS."

So.
There we have it.

I'm guessing that has something significant to do with all the lingering loneliness I feel, despite often wanting to be alone (even if I sometimes forget that I want to). It is always there in me somewhere, even when I feel solid and strong. The loneliness, the doubt, the fear—I have long struggled against these oppressors, and that is the thing of it, the whole notion of dancing with demons. To embrace them lovingly—what happens then? All the uncomfortable feelings. The ones I have struggled with my whole life—the ones I have hated in myself, have tried to hide, have tried to push away. The feelings that I've felt guilty about. The feelings which make me sure I must be less, I must be broken, I must be wrong...surely there must be something *wrong* with me.

Throughout my life I have drawn these experiences to myself again, and again, and again—experiences of unrequited love, of tragic beauty, of loss. I have kept myself in a perpetual state of *wanting* that which I'm not convinced is available to me, of never truly allowing myself to let it in. If I am creating my own realities, what am I creating, really? More uncertainty. I surround myself with beauty and integrity, then dare the Universe to snatch it away from me. What a truly goofy-ass thing to do.

This morning, I am smiling.

I look around at this fine townhouse. Here I live in Colorado, listening to the songs of my childhood on my dad's old stereo—John Denver, who put these beautiful dreams of mountains in my head. The visions, the feelings swirl in me, the creative force in me since I was a little girl. What I have also been creating for my entire lifetime. What I continue to create. In this vision today, I will ask myself (for the twenty-gazillionth time, but still) with today's eyes, and mind, and heart—

Tell me, my darling, my beautiful girl—
What do you choose to create?

Monday, January 11, 2021

A reminder to myself, in the guise of a letter to Beorn:

"We are more powerful than we give ourselves credit for. In every moment of every day, we have infinite choices to make… and I believe that what we choose is what we create.

Truly. In very real form.

I am practicing doing this consciously (it is certainly not what we're taught from birth). Whether we are doing it consciously or not, we are always creating what we choose. I am practicing creating wisdom, beauty, connection, health, growth, patience, prosperity, peace, compassion, light…

YOU are more powerful than you give yourself credit for.

Now you get to choose."

How then to reprogram what my brain and body have known for so long, that I may discontinue my patterns of reliving sadness, abandonment, isolation, and loss? So I may create for myself the experiences I desire and deserve? Experiences of security, joy, prosperity, connection, abundance, health, and peace. What is it that Loki said in that Avenger's film (or was it one of the Thor's)?

"I am burdened with glorious purpose!" he said.

And what is **my** purpose? To discover my strength, my balance, my joy. To allow myself to always be conscious of that warm inner light—or, at least, more often than not—to allow it to grow, and to flow. To radiate like the beams of sunlight at dawn, to spread nurturing beauty and bliss. All very airy-faerie, I suppose, but this is what I desire in my life. I see and feel the pain, the confusion, the imbalance, and upheaval in this world. I feel it so deeply, and it weighs on me. To remember how to take these burdens in stride, and to move on…to take the time that

I need for myself to rebalance and recharge. To keep learning and practicing what that looks like for me. To continue seeking guidance, wisdom, insight, and support. That is what I need. To allow myself to fully feel the immense and overwhelming *gratitude* which wells in me, for all the blessings in my life. To choose my path of Positivity. To allow for others who choose the same, and, rather than hiding myself away, to allow those like souls to join me.

There is so much in this Life.

I've decided to take (at least) a week-long fast from the Facebook, as, in my loneliness, I find it to be such a distraction, an unhealthy addiction playing itself out. Especially with my darling Fisher coming home from his dad's tomorrow, I really want to focus on the things that help me feel grounded, and in balance. Focus on eating healthy, on getting plenty of exercise, and outside time with the animals. Focus on reading, and writing good things, and yoga, and meditating. Focus on all that feeds my soul, rather than depleting it.

Then there is my other addiction, currently taking its shape in the form of the handsome Beorn. That is a distraction for me to take a break from, as well. I found myself sliding down its slippery slope again yesterday; obsessing and craving and throwing a little hissy fit in my mind, at the wanting what is being withheld from me. I literally saw an image of myself stomping my feet and shaking my fists like a frustrated three-year-old child. Wanting that toy so badly, and furious that its possession is out of my control. Super interesting. I find myself reaching out to him yet again, and again he does not reach back. It sounds preposterous when I write the words now, that I am still directing so much attention, so much energy, toward this idea of a something or someone when I don't even know what they are about, in actuality, and with whom there seems to be no balance in energy of intent.

For all the lovely ideas this man represents–those are wonderful; keep feeling those as what you are ready to embrace. For all the places where this three-dimensional being is not in a reality to step up to meet you, bless him still, and release your desire for him to be somewhere he is not. Decide if you wish to direct your energy to where it cannot be received. Decide if you wish to give your power and magic away.

Grow your love and your light, share it with those who also have their love and light growing. With others who wish to share. If you open your eyes and allow yourself to see clearly, you'll find it is everywhere.

Guide yourself gently back to Purpose, when you feel drawn toward these addictions, my dear. You have awareness, and you have help out there. You are doing so good. You are so good. You can stay this glorious course, blessed with Purpose, as you are.

At least I have been managing my animal addictions, if that is what you'd call them, though surely they come from a well-intended place. I am very conscious of not wanting to take on more than I can handle emotionally, financially, or energetically, as it goes without question that *every* creature deserves the highest quality of life. It is a question of being capable of meeting everyone's needs—and "everyone" includes me. We came **so close** to acquiring two rescued ferrets at Christmastime, but someone got dibs on them right before me. I have since put the ixnay on further notions of erretfays. I do find myself daydreaming from time to time, about adopting an Irish Wolfhound (because, with the social challenges of my PTSD from the dog attack, and Anzu's correlating issues with dog aggression, a ginormous rescued beast-dog would be exactly what we need). Then the other day I had this weird urge to adopt a kitten, of all things. WTF. Thankfully, that curious urge slipped away.

Right now, what I need to do is to get some warm clothes on and get Anzu out for a walk in the light of the rising sun.

Addiction is a curious thing, in all its many forms—as Ashaya trembles in my lap. One may have said that I didn't really need this adorable, traumatized little creature from among the dozens who were saved from the weird hoarding situation. But here she is, safe…and still trembling. Who knows what this little dog has to teach me, why she came to me. What I do know is that she seems to be a keeper.

Chapter 8
Letting the Journeys Begin

"There is this saying, 'Lovers don't finally meet somewhere,
they're in each other all along.'
I believe this to be true of our healing journey, as well.
It is not met or found somewhere or some place,
it is within us all along."

— Larson Langston

Friday, January 15, 2021

Last night I told Fish he could read for as long as he'd like to, as long as he brushed his teeth and took out his contacts before he went to bed. He came into my room to pluck little Ashaya from where she was nestled in front of me under the blankets. This created space for Anzu to lie right next to me, Shepherd face to my human face, my hand on her sternum, her paw over my arm. Where I could feel her breathing, feel her chest rise and fall. Where I could feel her whole warm body twitching in her sleep.

Glorious peace. Fulfillment.
(Remember this feeling.)
I will.

* * * * * *

It bears stepping away from my journal entries here, to share a bit about my history. For starters, I have never been one for experimenting with drugs, not even in my youth. Thankfully, as a highschooler, I ran with a crowd of Creatives; artists, musicians, punk-rockers, and the like, among whom declaring oneself to be "straight edge" (not partaking in alcohol, drugs, or casual sex, and supporting animal advocacy) was considered acceptable, if not cool. Just draw a black "X" on the back of your hands at a show and no one would try to pass a joint to you. On the rare occasion that I did smoke pot (cannabis, weed), I remember being so profoundly affected by it as to have sensations of sprouting thick hair all over my body (like an animal, no surprise), or of slipping through stairs and walls, no longer bound by the laws of three-dimensionality. My friends did not seem to share in my heightened sensitivities...So, yeah. Not so much of a thing for me, preferring to keep my body (more or less) hairless, and my feet (more or less) firmly in this dimension, on the ground.

In the late 1980s, when I was barely considered an adult, "Ecstasy" (now more commonly referred to as MDMA, or "Molly") came to my awareness by way of new college friends from the East Coast who knew of such exotica. These friends seemed unnervingly smart, beautiful, and "cool" to my self-doubting sensibilities, so when they insisted (well-intendedly) that I try the drug with them, it was hard to stand my ground in saying Thank You, but No. I remember Mateo telling me that if I didn't find it worth every penny of the $10 cost (no small sum to me at the time), that I didn't have to pay him back for it. I remember writing a check to him on the very next day, and the following weekend another check, so we all could do it again. It's true, the experience was like nothing I could have imagined. In the seeming sanctuary of the home of friends who I already admired for their collective charms, to call it "ecstasy" hardly begins to cover all that unfolded for our senses to explore (very innocently, sweetly)...I'll just leave it at that.

The problems began in earnest for me when the experience left the safe confines of our friends' home. I did ecstasy one more time with all of them, but this time we ventured out into the world of college party-town, Madison, Wisconsin. What had seemed sweetly intimate, innocent, and loving among friends now devolved to a scene which edged into debauchery. I found myself making-out with some pretty girl whose name I didn't know, and dangerously close to sleeping with a guy-friend. As my euphoria began to wane, I found Mateo in a dancing crowd, promising to pay him back for another dose, desperate to keep that high. The depth of anguish which eventually overtook me that night was like none I'd ever known. I remember leaving the bed of my friend (who I did not have sex with because we didn't have a condom—at least our wits were that much about us), sitting in a back stairwell which smelled of ancient wood, and seeing the sun begin to rise through an old window beside me. Tears poured down my face. I could hardly work my fingers to tie my boot laces, wracked with sadness as I was. I remember looking through the rippled old glass at the sunrise over the neighboring houses, thinking, how is it possible that the sun can even rise? How can this day even begin? Surely this was the end of the world…for me, at least, it felt like the end.

That was the last time I did ecstasy, though my friends continued to partake, from time to time. I was the sober one who accompanied my model-pretty girlfriend to parties, and pulled drunk guys away from her when she was too fucked-up to have discernment in her choices, combining alcohol with ecstasy out of a habit of drinking socially. I became known among my small group of friends as "The Ecstasy Queen," which I loved. It meant that when they were out toodeling around on their blissed-out quests, they'd come to my apartment so I could play Cocteau Twins records for them with their eyes closed, and dab honey from my fingertips to their lips. So I could tell them how lovely they were, and sing to them as I brushed their hair.

I don't remember when it was, exactly, but it was with that same group of friends that I did magic mushrooms, psilocybin.

That was the time I first became fully aware of the presence of spirits around me—the sensation I shared with my Nana that day at her dining room table. I'm trying to remember now what my take-away was exactly, but that was a long time ago. I do remember something coming up about my departed mother, but I think it was just a knowing that she was near. I remember, very pointedly, crawling up a flight of stairs in the old house, on my hands and knees—slowly, slowly—knowing that I would find God at the top of the stairs. I could hear voices up there, primarily the voice of the blonde-haired, blue eyed, Greek God of a fellow named Thad, speaking boldly, self-assuredly (I think about his sweaters). As I ascended the stairs on all fours, bound for divinity in its ultimate form, I closed my eyes, thinking, "Please don't let it be Thad...please don't let it be Thad..."

My hands reached the top step.

I opened my eyes to find Emmet the cat gazing down upon me knowingly.

"Meow," he said.

"Oh, Emmet, it's YOU!" I whispered, reaching up to scritch his neck, pressing my face into his scruff. I embraced him with palpable relief.

It made perfect sense.
Emmet also knew that he was God, as cats always do.

That first psilocybin experience opened a floodgate of insights that I really didn't know what to do with at the time. It was completely overwhelming, and I wasn't ready for it. I had no way (nor guidance) to process all of what the experience showed me, all of how it felt to me. One friend in our group freaked out and had to go to the ER to get his stomach pumped. My girlfriend (the model) just lay in bed, miserable, while her boyfriend tried to soothe her. She'd had good experiences on LSD, apparently (something I've not done to this day, though

I've tended friends on their trips), and moaned that mushrooms were probably just too "natural" for her.

I only tried mushrooms one other time, a few years later, when I was working as a garland-wench at the Colorado Renaissance Festival and dating the tall, handsome camel-handler, who played panpipes and looked amazing in my patterned tights. A friend of his gave us a handful of 'shrooms, and in hindsight it wasn't enough to have much effect, especially due to our collective heights—we were both quite tall for humans, though not so much for camels.

I remember walking around the quiet fairgrounds late at night, long after the patrons had left the festive town which stands waiting patiently year round. I remember thinking there were faeries having a dance party in my head, and I remember being super thirsty. When we finally came to the bubbler, I had the idea that I could just keep drinking while also taking a breath, because there's oxygen in water, and that's how fish breathe—very silly—so of course, I choked and sputtered the water out. I remember arguing with my camel-handler, as we often did, both being (besides tall) impassioned and opinionated souls. We bickered amongst the stoic evergreens and looming hills, we argued beneath the glorious moon and stars, beneath the unfathomable immensity of the sky. We both looked up just in time to see an asteroid streak across the darkness above the treetops, the mountains, the moon, and little, tiny us. We stood, silently, in awe. We turned to each other, and both agreed, we really shouldn't fight.

As I say, I have never tried LSD, and have no intention to. Just being around friends who were tripping, for all that entails, and for how long it lasts...it's always seemed like a can of worms that's best for me to leave unopened. It's a question I don't need answered, as the Black Widow says, when asked if she wants a try at lifting Mjölnir, the hammer of Thor. No Thor's hammer for me, either, thank you. I'll just stick to my regular ol' (curiosity of a) reality.

There was one time when my then teenaged sister and a girl-friend each took half a hit of acid, and were having a rough time of it. They showed up at my apartment (where I may have been playing Cocteau Twins records, and possibly The Cure), seeking some form of sanctuary or respite. I set them up at my kitchen table with crayons and coloring books. I remember sitting on my kitchen counter, legs dangling, eating Ben & Jerry's New York Super Fudge Chunk out of the tub, chatting with the gay beauty of a man who was living with me at the time (a whole 'nother story, I tell you). My sister and her friend looked content with their coloring, whispering and laughing amongst themselves. She would tell me later that her friend asked how I knew what to do for them in their altered state, and Wendy replied, "Because she's like this *all the time.*"

I loved that. I still love it. And maybe it's true. Since I've never done acid, I can't say from experience, but I do know that the veil between "realities" has always felt thin to me.

Now, hop skip and jump a couple decades forward, back where we left off with our story. The time where I'm living in Colorado with a beautiful teenaged child of my own, out among the mountains, the evergreens, and the falling stars which remind us not to fight. Living the Colorado dream, for all of its evolving shapes and forms…but it was beginning to feel like not *my* dream, anymore. Truth told, it felt like a nightmare, sometimes.

There was a span of time before the pandemic arrived when a lot of huge shifts were taking place—in the whole world, yes, and very much in my personal realm. Fisher and I had been living on a dreamy hobby farm that we loved, but the rent started going up, and up, and up. Within the span of a year, my old horse, my dad, my old dog, and my llama died. I ended up buying out my dad's townhouse from my sisters (the grown-up, responsible thing to do) and leaving our beloved hobby-farm life behind.

Important to this story's progression is when, a couple years earlier, I was attacked by the Great Pyrenees dog during a new-client interview, the psychological consequences of which rocked my world. Animals have always represented safety to me, in a reality where I can find human relationships challenging, at best, including, even, the relationship with my own child. With my mother having died when I was three years old, and my dad doing the best he could to manage his own troubles plus three little girls, I've long gravitated toward animals, perhaps missing out on some significant human social skills.

Great Pyrenees and German Shepherds have always been favorites of mine; many of the dogs I've been closest with in my lifetime have been variations on those themes. When Fisher was very young, I'd tell him a bedtime story about Govinda the Elder, the Livestock Guardian Dog who watched over the goat farm where I lived in Wisconsin for seven years. Govinda was a Maremma, an Italian breed, though much like a Great Pyrenees in appearance, nobility, and duty. Govinda was not a dog to be trifled with. He lived out back in the barn and fenced pastures with the horses, goats, llamas, and an angora sheep who often needed his bangs trimmed so he could see (Govinda stuck close to him). Though his thick, fluffy, cream-colored coat could tempt any dog-lover in for a big hug, Govinda did not like to be touched, or even looked at directly. He had a job to do, and he was very serious about doing it. If friends came to visit, and we were headed out to the barnyard to hang with the animals, I'd say simply, "Just put your hands in your pockets, don't look at him, and stay close to me. He's going to check you out, but you'll be fine." I was never the least bit afraid of Govinda, I just respected the boundaries he set. One afternoon, as he lay basking in the sun by the barn, I tried petting him… his eyes opened slightly and he let out a low, deep growl. I stopped immediately. I told him I was sorry, and respectfully moved away.

The story I told Fisher was of a night in the summertime, when, on a rare occasion, I got home after dark. I went out to the barn to say goodnight to my beloved goat, Patience, and became very concerned when I didn't find him in his usual sleeping place.

I called out into the darkness of night for him. "Patience! Patience, where are you? Patience!"

Way off in the distance, I heard the deep, rich sound—"Whooh whooh whooh whooh! Whooh whooh whooh whooh!" (I would lean in close to make this sound for Fisher)—of Govinda somewhere out there in the night.

"Whooh whooh whooh whooh!" he called.

I got my flashlight from the house and ventured out beyond the wooded trail, into rolling pastures, following the sound—"Whooh whooh whooh!"—and as I neared the backside of the 40-acre property, where the fence line reached the pine forest where the coyotes lived, I could see Govinda's ghostly white form rising to stand and his tail wagging, so happy that I had arrived.

"Here! Here he is!" Govinda showed me. Patience had gotten his head stuck through the fence. From the looks of the trampled grass beneath his hooves, it seemed he had been stuck for hours. Patience bleated anxiously as I got his head and horns free. I told Govinda what a very good boy he was as he stood by, overseeing my work. The three of us ventured back to the farm together by the light of the flashlight, awash in our collective relief.

Govinda the Elder held such a special place in my heart, though my relationship with him was very different than with any dog I had known. When he passed of old age the spring before I ended up moving to Colorado, it was heartbreaking. I adopted a cream-colored, soulful puppy later that winter from the shelter where I worked. He had ice-blue eyes and looked like the white German Shepherd I had dreamed of having as a child, though his ears eventually flopped as he matured. I named him Govinda in honor of my lost guardian and friend, and the name felt deeply fitting—Govinda, the Companion and Protector (in the story of Siddhartha, companion to the young Buddha). Govinda the Younger lived for nearly fourteen years and was absolutely my angel dog. Even now it is difficult to think of him, for how much I miss him, for what a dear and unique presence he was in my life. He was a year older than Fisher, born the same month, and I'm sure had a great influence on Fisher's affinity for dogs. Govinda raised Anzu, my Shepherd-mix Rez puppy, whom I brought home unknowingly with Parvo virus (the killer of so many Reservation dogs). They became the best of friends. Anzu always respected Govinda, in fact, I dare say her sun rose and set by him. She bowed down to him submissively, lovingly, as she has done for no other dog. I know Anzu still misses Govinda, as I do. I can feel that she does.

So, yeah. The huge, beautiful, "protector" dog biting the holy hell out of my legs opened up a giant can of suppressed "old trauma" worms, many that I wasn't yet conscious of. Following that experience, all the loss coming my way within the next couple of years was going to serve up a whole bunch more worms.

So, let the worm-wrangling begin.

All that is to say, around the time of my first involvement with Beorn, I was in a pretty vulnerable state. I was trying to get my bearings, to get my sea legs from all the Life Changes which felt so profound. I have long struggled with significant bouts of depression and anxiety, and living in the countryside with animals has been my soothing balm. Moving to a townhouse was difficult for me, lovely townhouse though it may be. There are just too many humans around and not enough outdoor space for the animals, or me. I still miss hearing owls hoo-hooing at night, and waking up to find my old llama, Sebastian, sleeping feet away, beneath my bedroom window. I dare say I have adjusted much better to townhouse living these days, but at the time, I struggled significantly. In times of normal age-appropriate conflicts between us, the teenaged darling and heart of my heart could push me easily over the edge, into frightening fits of tears and rage. I spent days lost in feelings of debilitating loneliness and lack of purpose, peppered with thoughts of suicide. If it weren't for the needs of the animals and the boy, there were many days I would not have gotten out of bed. To top it all off, after the attack, my fear of new dogs escalated out the roof, putting me on perpetual high alert. I was constantly in a state of fight or flight, with most of my income at the time derived from walking dogs. It came to the point where I remember feeling that I was either going to become a shut-in, kill myself (definitely not an option for the sake of my son, if no other, not to mention my dogs and the cat. The fish would probably be fine without me.) or figure out how to get some very serious help.

Thankfully, my best-bestie was in therapy for PTSD after being buried and nearly killed by a back-country avalanche—her partner located and dug her out just as she was losing consciousness. She told me about a new modality referred to as "psychedelic-assisted psychotherapy" for the treatment of anxiety, depression, and PTSD. While the idea of doing psychedelics was not remotely appealing to me, I was at my wits end. I learned that there were underground avenues for exploring psychedelic therapy, which included a traditional talk therapy approach, IFS (Internal Family Systems) "parts" work, somatic healing therapy, some energy work, as well as the eventual use of psychedelics. I had several sessions with a counselor *just talking* before we even discussed what sort of "Medicine Journey" might be helpful for me. There was a lot of "getting to know you" to do, a whole lot of trust to be built in our working relationship, and for me, bucket-loads of crying, too. I am talking skid-steer-sized bucket-loads of crying.

Which brings us to the documentation of my Work, by which I mean all of my personal healing work, and very importantly, my Journeys. A "Journey," in my case, is the term for a day-long intensive therapy session in which some form of psychedelic is administered to basically guide the way. I've listened to loads of podcasts on this subject, I've read Michael Pollan's book *How to Change Your Mind*, and I've watched the Netflix documentary series. From what I hear and read, it seems to me that the clinical research of these compounds is advancing in leaps and bounds, and hopefully the legality of public use in controlled therapies will catch up with its medicinal potential.

Obviously, I am not a medical professional in any way, I am just someone who happened upon these medicines and this work, and I would like to share my (ongoing) story with you, dear reader. Furthermore, this is my opportunity to revisit my journals from those times; as I've mentioned, I have not read them in entirety since they were written. For me this is an exciting undertaking, and also daunting—to revisit the angels, the demons, the profundity of those times, both the actual Journeys and all the work in between. To try to share this all with you, if it is even possible with words.

As always, I assure you, I will do the best that I can.

Chapter 9
Setting Out Toward the First Journey

"Until one is committed, there is hesitancy, the chance
to draw back, always ineffectiveness. Concerning all acts
of initiative (and creation), there is one elementary truth,
the ignorance of which kills countless ideas and splendid
plans: that the moment one definitely commits oneself,
then Providence moves, too. All sorts of things occur to
help one that would never otherwise have occurred. A
whole stream of events issues from the decision, raising in
one's favour all manner of unforeseen incidents and meet-
ings and material assistance, which no man could have
dreamed would have come his way."

— W.H. Murray, *Scottish Himalayan Expedition*

Before we dive back in, I must confess that I've reached another
struggling point in this writing.

There are just *so many words* in my journals. It's difficult to
know exactly which passages to draw from, which are important
for the purposes of this storytelling, and which are going to be
unhelpful, or overkill. I look at my notes from my first Journey
on March 4th of 2021, held at the homestead of friends way out

in the country, where my dogs and I stayed with their elderly Rhodesian Ridgeback, Tigger. I have my counselor's transcripts to draw from, though it can't be easy to take detailed notes and still be present for your client who is tripping balls, for whatever that looks like for them. I find some of the notes now difficult to follow. It seems such a shame to lose wisdom which comes from these unique mental, spiritual, and very emotional excursions. It might seem worthwhile to sound-record or even videotape the entire day of journeying, but would doing so impede on the sanctity of the experience? I don't know. Right now, I feel daunted by the task of making sense of and organizing all the notes in a way that will also make sense to others, while not dragging this out into a tediously multi-volumed affair.

To keep it concise and relevant, that is my goal, while not losing sight of the magical, whimsical embellishments of fancy, which also make the story worthwhile. Just like life, I reckon. There does need to be lots of room for magic, and whimsical embellishments of fancy. Otherwise, truly, what would be the point? Also, you'll note from the dates of journal entries I've chosen to share, what feels relevant to my actual Journeywork can be far-reaching.

When we get to the actual Journey day, I thought about straight-up copying my counselor's notes, but it definitely requires translation. Unfortunately, while under the sway of the medicine, I don't believe I'd be capable of writing in my own hand. Brandi and I have laughed about how, if we were to try writing while Journeying, the extent of our scribbles would be something along the lines of, "*Saaaaaaad….*"

Another thing that I've learned is that this Journeywork truly begins well before ever taking the medicine. I mean *weeks* before. For this reason, it's important to become clear on what one's "intentions" are for a Journey—what wisdom or insights one is seeking, what it is you wish to address, heal, or change in yourself—because the Universe will get to work on those intentions straight away.

Then you have your actual Journey with the medicine, which can be intense, powerful, insightful…and tremendously uncomfortable, at times. For me, it always seems to involve some form of purging—mostly crying, wailing, sobbing. Sometimes throwing up. I've found myself laying there, miserable, thinking, I just paid a bunch of money to basically give myself the stomach flu.

But the actual day of medicine-work is just the opening of a doorway, really. Once you've stepped through to the other side, even after the medicine wears off, the shifts in perception and belief begin to take place, a new wisdom begins to nestle in. These shifts can feel immediate and profound, or they can feel very gradual. Often they are a combination of each. This is when neuroplasticity is the most profound, I understand, offering the greatest opportunity for "rewiring"—hence, it is extremely important to be conscientious of what influences one has during this time.

In my experience, the Spirit of the Journey begins working in earnest a couple of weeks before the date set for my Intensive, through lots of big feelings, "coincidences," and observations, and especially through words poured into my journals. Then, in the days, weeks, and months beyond a Journey, long after the medicine has left the fibers of my physical body, the insights continue to unfold. The neural wiring continues to realign. My writings end up being as much a factor in my process as anything, both before and after the actual Journeys—I honestly don't know how people fully absorb this work without the help I find from these written outpourings, long-winded as mine may be. It's like having a therapist in spirit who is with me all the time, asking questions, giving prompts, sorting through all these thoughts and insights over coffee every morning. Taking really effing good notes.

* * * * * *

Monday, January 18, 2021

...there is this idea of changing your *THOUGHTS*—of recognizing that thoughts in themselves are fully creative, just as words and actions are creative, it all begins with one's thoughts.

I have lived with so many thoughts tumbling through my head, like a herd of cats—unruly, uncontrollable. With no apparent direction to their frenzied scrambling. Often dark and broody, these cats of mine can be frightened, insecure, unsure. All the wiring of my troubled youth, all the programming which still influences a tremendous part of my mind, consciously or (mostly) unconsciously. All that does not serve me, which I strive to rewire and relearn.

"THINK GOOD THOUGHTS," as stated on a bumper sticker I found in Berkely, California, in my early days of gypsy traveling. When something does not serve the greater good of All (or of the moment, or of the Self, connected), some say to simply *Change Your Mind.*

It does seem so basic, so simple, right? Yet it is not at all what has been hard-wired in me, nor seemingly in most of our culture. That's okay, that is part of our learning, our growing, our evolution, our experience of Life as a part of this physicality. This is what we are here for, each and every one of us. For me, I reckon it begins with Me. The ripples I create flow out from my center, just as everyone else's ripples flow to me. What do I choose to create, to share? And how do I choose to receive?

Find your center.
Radiate from there.
Choose what you create.

These thoughts tumbling through my mind like so many cats...so, what is the solution? Not to try to continue herding them chaotically, it would seem. Rather, to pause, to be still, to breathe here in this place. To set down some saucers of warm milk, widely dispersed so all may partake. Let those cats gather 'round the sustenance, let them hunker in. Let them lap at it with their prickly tongues, that I may call to them in a sing-songy voice, that I may draw one at a time into my lap. These thoughts, these cats—let me caress them, let me soothe them, one by one. Let me hold them gently, to discover their wisdom, their peace, their grace.

Sunday, February 28, 2021
4:35 a.m. or so

It is ever so important, oh, darling girl, to focus on what feels Right to Me. Right now, what feels Right seems to be a whole lot of mucking around in the mire. So be it. Muck away.

Joan loaned me a book during our counseling session the other day, the day when I was again full of crying and anger and resistance to even talking with her, resistance to all this bullshit of trying to trust people, anyway. Just thinking about it now makes the heat rise in me in a wave of nausea, makes moisture spring from my pores to all of my skin, to my brow. Call them hot flashes, call them power surges or whatever—call them what you will. They are intense, uncomfortable, and undoubtedly have a message for me, just in that. So, what is the message, already? I remove my oversized fleece jacket, the one that doesn't like to stay buttoned anyway. I let it fall around me where I sit. I close my eyes, inhale deeply through my nose, raise my chest, straighten my spine up toward the sky. Ah, *this*. What is your message, Uncomfortableness? No words. The heat, the hot dew on my skin subsides.

Breathe.
Just Breathe.
In and out. Deeply.
Now, *open your eyes.*

Outside the (aptly named) picture window of this home where I'm caretaking, the picture I see is this: faintly, in the darkness, mountains like sleeping giants, darkness and greys and deep blues, layers of wild and crisp winter night. Of the sleepy, still breath of the Earth. Of all the Spirits, the Wisdom, the All. Out there across the countryside, I know there is so much going on that I don't see—the animals among the pinon trees, the humans out further still, the multitude of individual realities expanding into eternity.

...and yet, dial it back in, my dear, to the impression of those sleeping mountains, to the impression of those trees. Dial it back in to this, your dream. To the sound of your friend's old dog breathing from

his enormous chest, on the bed in the room behind you. To the sound of the refrigerator hum. Now. Start right here. What is right around you, and in front of you? Start counting your blessings, right here.

> *Bless them,*
> *and let them go.*
> *And bless them,*
> *and let them go.*

Because that is the thing of it, remember? The lesson you've been followed by quietly your whole life. It has yet to fully sink in. The lesson is not that "Life's Not Fair," as Dad used to growl through the gnashed teeth of his own frustration—unless that's what you want it to be. *The lesson is not that "Love Equals Loss," like the banner above your head*—unless that's what you want it to be. *The list can go on and on, about fear and pain and uncertainty, about loneliness and lack of purpose. If that is what you choose as your wisdom,* then so be it—*there are plenty who will agree. But, oh, my darling, are you cut from that cloth? Is that what feels Good and Right for you? You who feels* absolutely everything *so deeply—will you take it as your blessing, or your curse?*

You who feels as though you must be from another freakin' planet or something, because surely you have never quite fit in here. With all the words and the judgements, the gimme-gimmes and supposed-to-bes. All of the noise and anger and care-less-ness. All the hurting of each other, if it means getting MORE. More THINGS for the gimme-gimmes, rather than more peace, more balance, more love.

That, oh, darling girl, is not what I choose. It is not what I choose for me—to carry with me, to present in every moment as my gift to the world. And it is not the gift that I choose to receive.

*So, tell me, then...**what will it be?***

The book Joan loaned me is *How to Change Your Mind*, by Michael Pollan.

And again, I hear a whisper of the always, forever question: *WHAT DO YOU CHOOSE TO CREATE IN THIS DREAM?*

Tuesday, March 2, 2021
4:47 a.m.

I have been sleeping pretty well out here in the vast coun-tryside, it's true. I mean, I still wake up in the night drenched in sweat, having to throw the covers off, or sometimes having to get up to use the loo. Maybe sometimes Ashaya's little toenails are poking into my skin, and I need to reposition her…but all told, I am sleeping well. I go to bed with a book not long after sunset, as there's nothing out here to watch a movie on, which is actually just fine with me. There will be time to watch movies when I am no longer staying here. For now, I would rather watch the sun set beyond those fourteeners, through the giant picture window, by the crackling of the wood stove fire, with a cup of tea in hand. For now, I would rather fill my mind with the words of a good book until my eyelids begin to droop, regardless of the time; to turn the bedside lamp off and sleep when my weary mind tells me to. Yes, indeed, that suits me just fine. To rise in the morning when my body tells me it's done resting, to slip on slippers and shuffle out into the kitchen, across the beautiful old wooden floors. To start the kettle. To wish the moon Good Morning. To hear the dogs sighing on the bed from which I just rose.

All feels Right, and Well and Good. All in my little world.

Yesterday morning I came upon the Arcturian Group Message from February 28, which had been hidden away under "promotions" in my email (sure, okay, although helpful messages from Light Beings out there somewhere in the Multiverse seem like a worthwhile promotion to me). What I found most helpful in the message was the emphasis on personal relationships, and addressing all the shifts going on, particularly at this time both personally and in our world. It made me think of my old friend Lee in Arizona, and of his recent unforeseen divorce. It made me think of my comment to him when we spoke Sunday evening, when he mentioned how they'd forbidden their daughter from dating until she was sixteen, and how she'd been just fine with that. I told Lee how even when I was a little girl, I'd always felt highly driven to find my partner in life—maybe he would be a boy out running with a pack of dogs in the woods, like me (I started my first dog-walking service when I was eleven years old, so Hoyt Woods was where you'd often find me). But here I am literally decades down the road, I said to Lee, and you can see how that has panned out. It's interesting. I do wonder what's up with that.

The Arcturian message spoke of our human notion that we need to find our "other half" in life, when, in fact, the long and short of it is, we are already fully whole. It is interesting to me that I've spent so much energy in my lifetime—so much thought, so much emotion—attempting to curb my own wretched loneliness by stuffing other beings into that perceived hole. I attempt to fill the void with animals, with humans, and often with food, trying to satiate that longing, trying to make the sadness leave. It can get mighty crowded in there, while still not satisfying the need. Distractions may bring temporary respite, but ultimately the longing and loneliness do not go away. The methodology makes sense only in that it is what was modeled to me from early childhood, through television, through music, and through my dad. I watched my dad struggle with his own emptiness after losing my mother, watched him disparately try to fill that gaping hole with relationships, with money, with appearances, with food. With trying to maintain some sort of control over life, and a façade of being the man he thought others expected him to be.

So, there we have it. Awareness can lead to change. These lessons circling around me for years and years and years, these helpful little ideas which have rung true somewhere in me, they now ring more brightly, clearer. I am paying attention, I am watching, I am listening. I am working on it, by golly, I am.

All is well, and as it should be.

* * * * * *

First Medicine Journey
Thursday, March 4, 2021
MDMA
Intention: Exploration of anger, fear, father/mother, dogs

I was awake, as usual, before sunrise the morning of my Journey, writing in my journal, having coffee. I had one client horse to tend before I could settle in and let the day be entirely about me, and I wrote of feeling a little resentful, while also understanding that there really was no other way—the owner had to leave town for an emergency surgery for her husband, and I was the only person they had (or trusted?) to care for their elderly horse. Ultimately, I think I was just fussing a little, playing out the story of, "It falls to me to take care of everyone else, but there's no one to take care of me!" That is fine, if that's what I needed to feel that morning. I would get over it, eventually. And it was good for my heart to see that old horse. Especially considering the day I had ahead of me, the Horse energy was very well timed.

According to the Journey notes written by Joan, I took the medicine at 9:50 a.m. We did an opening ceremony, burning sage, and asking for guidance from and expressing gratitude to the directions—North, South, East, West, to the sky above us, and to the earth below. I settled in comfortably on the sofa, facing the picture window and the mountains off to the west of Tigger's home. I read a journal entry out loud to Joan, the one about the lessons of life, of it being "Not fair," of Love equaling Loss, and how we get to choose. We spoke about these ideas for some twenty minutes or so before I began to get sleepy and hunkered in.

According to the notes, I said to Joan, "I don't think I've ever been nurtured. I can't ask for nurturing until I know I'm enough." This was the medicine beginning to kick in, and the amygdala shutting down, going to sleep. The amygdala is the part of our brain where all our fears and "threatening stimuli" are processed. It is necessary and helpful to us when there are actual threats at hand, but can be decidedly unhelpful when trying to access and work through old trauma. This is the part of our psyche where our "protectors" reside, the parts of us who tend to resist, and to shut out painful memories. In my IFS work with Joan, I began referring to my protector as "the Fuck You guy." The part in me that was quick to anger, to push back when under duress, emotional or otherwise. When the MDMA kicks in in earnest, my protector goes to sleep. The notes say that I "went inward," lying silently on the sofa. Then, as the first huge wave of emotion surged through me, I remember raising my hands to my face and wailing, "I miss my Mom..."

This is when I began to cry, and cry. I'm pretty sure I cried for the better part of the rest of the day.

"I can't believe I ever did this recreationally," I said, awash with all the feelings.

"It's a whole different intention," Joan replied.

I held Ashaya close to me, like a baby. "This is why I don't smoke pot," I said with my eyes still closed, "It makes me feel..." then overwhelmed by another wave of emotion, crying, "I want my Momma, I want my Mom..." I cradled Ashaya and began saying, "It's okay, baby, it's okay..." These words became a mantra throughout the day, repeated in a sing-songy tone.

"She's like the little baby me," I told Joan, petting and kissing Ashaya. "It's why she frustrates me sometimes."

I spoke of Mindy, our poodle when I was a little girl, how I pretended Mindy was my mother. But then Mindy had to die, too, one horrible night of being banished to the basement, after my dad spanked her for being incontinent. I remember how enormous his hand looked against her small, frail form, and I remember crying. I found her cold body early in the morning, tucked under a shelf, on the concrete floor.

Joan asked if the little girl in me wanted to be held.

"I don't think I've ever had that," I said. "I feel like I've always been alone, but I don't like being alone."

At about noon, the notes show that I was talking about Fisher, about how I became a mom. "But Fisher didn't want to come out," I sighed. He was born eventually by c-section, after a long and grueling labor. He never did make it to the birth canal.

I spoke of how Anzu feels like she needs to protect me because she knows I'm afraid, but she leaves when I get angry, because she's afraid that she's not safe. It is the same with Fisher, I said to Joan. "When I get angry, he gets scared that he's not safe, he doesn't know that I could never hurt him. I want him to feel safe...I want him to feel safe...but I get overwhelmed, I get so scared, and I get so angry. I lose control of that energy. It happens so, so fast. Anzu's worried for me because she sees how afraid I am," I said. Then the sing-song began, as though another wisdom spoke through me. "It's okay, baby...you're okay, Momma...it's okay, baby, you're safe. You can let this go, little girl, you can let this go..." I cooed to myself, motioning with my hands as though waving them gently through water. "It's okay, baby girl, you're safe. You're safe."

I spoke again about Anzu. "It's hard for her because she wants to be my protector. And she misses Govinda—he was never afraid of me, he just gave me space. He felt tenderness for me, let me wrestle with my own demons. He removed himself because he was wise. Fisher goes to his Dad's house now when I get angry and he doesn't feel safe, but my anger is not really about him. I love him so much...How do I feel safe?" I asked Joan.

"See if you can ask that question," she said gently, "and listen for the answer inside."

The notes said it was about one in the afternoon, and they become a little jumbled, as I'm sure there was a lot going on. The notes say that we talked about trusting life, and allowing things to unfold. There's something about a house full of rescue dogs, and anxiety coming up in my chest, and me clearing the energy with a motion of my hands. Something about trying not to be in conflict with my thoughts. Ashaya laying on my belly, I was breathing deeply and releasing, letting the energy flow on its own. Then she appeared to me, the one I have come to know as Light Momma, a maternal being or energy, which feels like pure light and love (she began coming to me in meditations before my first Journey, filling me with such joy. She looks a bit like a stereotypical "alien" form, with an oval face and almond-shaped eyes, and long, elegant fingers shimmering light). She came to my mind's eye in the Journey, saying, "It's only pain, a body sensation." Touching, tapping my face gently with her long, light fingers, cooing, "It's okay, you're safe."

"She is the part of me that is connected to my mother," I said to Joan. "I forget, but she's always there. Like her spirit is out there… but would be better if she were inside…" I reach my arms out, then back to pat my chest. "Come here, Momma…" I began to cry.

"It seems she has really been present here today," said Joan.

"Anzu is like me in dog form," I said. "Strong, beautiful, feral. She has a hard time trusting. She gets angry, and scared. I love her so much. She feels safe here, with us."

There was some talk about the Great Pyrenees who attacked me, about how it wasn't her fault. She and the other Pyrenees had been stuck in a camper for far too long; she had been anxious, and was trying to protect her space. I compared her to Govinda the Elder at the goat farm in Wisconsin, who'd had a job to do. Aspen had been taken away from her land in the countryside and now wasn't sure what her job was. "I wasn't very comfortable with the owner lady," I said. The animals had felt safe to me at first, but the person did not; she seemed stressed-out, and erratic.

I was rocking back and forth as I spoke of the attack; when Joan asked about the rocking, I told her, "It feels good."

There are notes about my dad, about the time when he was on his death bed (literally) and I was so angry with him about some things he said and did that day. Even on his last day in his body on this earth, our personal challenges continued. I had sought refuge in his walk-in closet, tears streaming down my face, in a fury of confusion, sadness, and rage. I called out for my mother to help me, please—and immediately heard her reply in my mind. "He is having a hard time," she said. "He is a scared little boy."

The notes went on: "It wasn't my dad's fault when I was a little girl, but still I was hurt. I couldn't trust my dad, and my mother had to leave, had to die." I didn't want to feel anger at my dad (Joan notes, "big emotion")...the anger protected the little girl. A black-and-white image (a photo I'd brought for the Journey) of five-year-old me, little girl, dressed in overalls and a striped shirt, leather shoes with shoelace untied, messy hair and mud on her hands. She holds a worm out to her father, it has been pulled in two—the little girl didn't mean to hurt the worm and feels very badly. She is asking her father if he can fix the worm, if he can glue it back together...but he takes a photograph instead. "Her daddy doesn't understand," I said.

Three o'clock in the afternoon, and I was saying, "I don't want to need—I begrudge that fact; I don't want to need someone." Even if someone doesn't end up being a crazy-person, eventually I will still lose them. Even the animals, like my beloved soul-mate dog, Camille, who was born on my twentieth birthday. "We lose them," I said to Joan. "I had her put to sleep because she had dementia, and a bleeding tumor at the base of her tail which would not heal. She was scared all the time, because of the dementia. Letting her go was the kindest thing to do, but it was too painful. I turned my emotions to my other dogs, to Joey (my Rat Terrier), and Zeek (my handsome Husky/Hound). I was so in love with Zeek. All of my emotions from Camille went into Zeek...it was the worst."

Within months of putting Camille to sleep, Zeek ran off into the wintery woods of our country home, chasing after some deer. His body was found a nightmarish two months later by hunters in the woods of neighboring land. His beautiful body was perfectly preserved by the cold, his head stuck into a hole in a log, as if he had chased some critter in there. "He went out with his boots on," as the saying goes. He had probably frozen to death, as it was bitterly cold. I was devastated, to say the least.

The notes said: "I carved out a life where I wouldn't need anyone, which felt free, but I also wanted a partner to join me. Like a catch-22. I was safe, but horribly lonely. Any time I met someone they were drawn to my independence, but when I showed needs or vulnerability, they'd run. I don't blame them. I never felt safe. I'd be too tapped into fear, or I would find fault with them and find an excuse to leave them first. These protectors guard my vulnerable heart.

"My basic belief is that I'm not safe. Even when my dad hit us, I know he loved us. I guess what I learned is that love is not safe. But he tried his best."

Joan: "Go inside to see what you notice."

"I'm remembering the Shaman workshop on the river [when Fisher was just a toddler] when all the anger and sobbing came raging out of nowhere. The Shamen held space for me, made a circle around me with arms spread wide as I bellowed and beat my fists on the wooden boards of their porch, until I had gotten it out. I felt completely wrecked and exhausted, like I do now. (*Going inward...tears.*)

"I keep having images of Govinda the Elder—I don't know why I'm crying. It's okay, old man, it was time (*tears, memories of finding the elder Govinda's body in the barn, as if he'd gone to sleep*). It was so sad. He helped me with the goats, and the time he stayed by Patience when his head was stuck in the fence. Govinda protected Patience—that was his job. He was so happy to see me! He was loyal, protective. I have a painting of Govinda now, he is the protector of our house. Aspen looked so much like him...maybe that's why it felt like such a betrayal? Govinda was so special, I miss him."

(I may have been speaking of either or both Govindas, there.)

"When I get scared, I don't know what to do. I get angry and confused, I feel victimized."

Joan: "Maybe ask inside and see what feeling anger has to show you."

"Anger at feeling weak, vulnerable…the words are 'toughen up' or you'll be scared, and when you're scared you will get hurt. (Joan's note: *this is a protector and its belief.*) I feel vulnerable even just walking dogs, like I might get hurt. I heard a woman calling her dog out on the trail, imagined the worst things that could happen. I felt helpless…*(turning inward)*. It's my dad barreling down the hallway, and we girls wondering who he's after, who is going to get hurt. He would come out swinging. That's why Fisher gets scared, he feels that fear, that rage. He feels like I'm going to hurt him, even though I never would. He still feels the rage in me, the pain pouring out on him. I'm sure it must be terrifying."

(I am so sorry, Fisher.)

"I noticed when my dad was dying that his hands looked small and frail. He needed me to hold his hand. When I was younger, I only dated men with long hair and who were slender, almost feminine in stature. 'Man hands' to me were scary."

Joan's note:
"Protector came back 'online' as medicine began to wear off [and, man, he was really not happy]—noticed as nauseousness, belief that he can't trust—'NO!'—pushing people away. Building awareness and appreciation of this part and how it helps keep Laura safe from being overwhelmed.

"Ceremony closed at 5 p.m."

* * * * * *

Friday, after dark.

You're okay, baby.
You're okay, Momma.

Over and over and over again, with gentle fingertips touching my face, caressing and tapping my skin so lightly, stroking my hair...*You're okay, baby, you're okay, Momma*...so soothing, and nurturing in that touch.

Saturday, March 6, 2021
6:45 a.m.

The sun rises and glows orange into the master bedroom, pours in through the glass of the back door and the modest windows all around the east and south walls. It is so beautiful here, and I will not want to leave on the morning of the eleventh, though our lonely cat will surely be grateful to have me home.

Yesterday I walked the nature trail with Brandi and spoke loudly in my excitement; I laughed, and cried, and paused, having to crouch because my body was tired of standing. I still felt all stoney-baloney through a good part of the day, and felt like I probably shouldn't drive, but had that old mare, and our Apollo and aquariums, to tend. I canceled a walk with a client dog who could do without me, saying simply that I wasn't feeling well, though that absolutely was not it. I drove carefully, focusing with great diligence, smiling and laughing at myself in my sweet grinning shimmer. Everything still seemed so stunningly beautiful, crisp, ALIVE. I wondered how long this feeling could last, if it could possibly go on forever, minus the stoney, shaky, tired bits. My body felt as though I'd spent most of the previous day throwing up. It is not far from true, really, along with the not eating much throughout the day (I remember being barefoot on the wooden boardwalk outside, savoring a tiny wedge of orange—the succulent taste of the tiniest nibble, the surprisingly sensual feel of it on the tip of my tongue), and the purging, purging, purging. Then the moments of peace, and resting, and comfort, and being nurtured when I needed it. "I'm right here," Joan's voice said to me gently from somewhere nearby, my eyes covered by my fingers and hands, "I am right here with you." Then the rise again of that wretched, awful pain, the wailing, the sobbing, the tears...

Oh, my darling, you are beautiful as tears–

Those words echoed in my head all day yesterday. *You are beautiful as tears.*

I do not wish to worry anyone, I do not wish to frighten Anzu and Ashaya over there on the sofa, after having to tell Ashaya more than once, calmly but firmly, "No, my sweet, I am sorry. I need you not in my lap this morning, because finally, I need to write." I need to write. I need to sort through all these many feelings, this jumbled outpouring of emotion from when that dam busted loose.

It took a few hours for my protectors to build it back up again, to get it back to a reasonable wall to guard. *You may have only this much trickle of emotion from me,* my Protector says. *You may have only this much vulnerability.* The swells rise and want to bust loose, it will surge like a wave of sadness and apprehension and fear...I don't know what to do with this, I think, these feelings are much too large, unruly and untamed. These waves will be the death of me, don't you think?

"Well, I know what to do with them!" my Protector chimes in. He is strong, he is willful. He tends those walls well. He draws the waves, the gushing floods back in. He contains them securely behind those walls.

Oh, my darling, you are beautiful, as tears—

I wonder how long this will go on, this ebb and this flow. This intensity. These parts of me, unleashed fully for the few hours, before Protector was able to begin reining it all back in. Is this still an altered state, or is this now who I am?

Well, my darling, tell me—who do you choose to be?

I feel myself trembling.

*It's okay, Momma, it's okay, baby girl...*Light Momma comes to me, touches my face, my neck, my hair gently. She whispers these words to me, the words that came through me for what may have been hours and hours on Thursday, when the dam was busted down and I was both, and ALL, and free to flow with everything. **Every Thing.** The pain, and the beauty, and the Understanding. I was a'flow with it all *(sweet baby, darling child)*, I was a part of it All.

I get scared when the fear comes flowing back in, or when it rises in me, or wherever it comes from. I want to push it away, I want it gone—I cower in a ball, and I sob. I wrapped myself around darling Ashaya, baby girl; I protected her as she played the part of Me—she knows that role well, to feel vulnerable, frightened, alone. Not knowing who to trust, or how to escape, she puts her trust in me, she surrenders her fear to me. My God, what a gift, this beautiful baby girl. To allow me to cradle her and drench her soft head with my tears. To soak it all in, and allow this, as though she has let go of something which I have not yet allowed myself to. "It's okay, baby girl. You're okay, Momma…" Tentatively, sometimes, but ultimately she lets go. She lets herself be safe with me.

Ah, yes. SAFETY.

This is the big one. This is why Anzu watches me so closely. She is so tuned in to me, in all my tumbling through waves of strength and vulnerability. She wants to protect me, she is my guardian feminine Angel Dog. She is not like my Protector, who resides in a stern masculinity. She is a Warrior who resides in deep emotion and compassion, who becomes frightened and uncertain when she doesn't know how to protect me. This is why she leaves when she feels the energy of my temper begin to rise. This part of me frightens her and makes her feel insecure, cowardly, and ashamed that she can no longer protect me. Just like Fisher, the intensity of my rage feels too huge, too unpredictable. When the sting of its intensity lashes out toward them, it feels unbearable—in those moments I become a terrifying monster, not Mother. Not a nurturer or protector. Not me. I understand that the only thing to do in those moments is to run away, to try to hide until that monster leaves. I understand Anzu, Fisher, because once upon a time that frightened child was me. The monster was my father, with spit and rage and pain, thundering down the hallway to come and get me. Coming to hurt that little baby girl, lost in the wretched fury of his own rage, and pain.

It's okay, Momma.
It's okay, baby girl.
It's okay, Poppa...you are also beautiful
      as tears.

THIS is a big one.

This one I did not expect, somehow, though it would seem obvious as it has lingered around the edges. I have not been willing to look at it, it has been too frightening to see. Oh, my poppa, my sweet little baby boy—you, my darling father. You are beautiful as tears, too. If I can forgive and find peace with that terrifying monster in you, perhaps I can forgive and find peace with that terrifying monster in me, too. Then perhaps I won't have to be afraid anymore. Perhaps I can truly learn to Trust (oh, my Lord) and feel Safe. Is that even possible?

Yes.

Then perhaps those others most beloved to me can learn to Trust and feel Safe with me, too.

Now, Ashaya in my lap sighs deeply, nestles in. Anzu watches me from the sofa across the room. She relaxes, closes her eyes. When I began to wail at this realization, when Mother Light showed me gently again as she did that day in the closet when Daddy was trying to ready himself to die—he is just a frightened little boy, she said to me then. He is so scared, too.

It's okay, Poppa...it's okay, darling baby boy.
It's okay, Momma, you are safe.
It's okay, my darling baby girl...you are beautiful, as tears.

I was afraid the dogs would leave me then, I was afraid they would be frightened by my loud wails...but, no, they both slid from the sofa and came to me; as I crouched on the floor, they came to my mourning embrace. Anzu's tail wagged gently as she licked the tears from my face, my throat, my eyes—so nurturing, so beautiful, so strong, so wise. Ashaya raised herself up on hind legs to be nearer to me, she wiggled, and her tiny toenails pressed my skin pointedly. Sweet little baby girl—this is how she shows her support to me, trembling and smiling sheepishly. She is present, my lil' baby girl. They are both right here with me. I smile, I laugh, I feel so relieved. I feel in awe of their incredible beauty, these creatures, like furry beams of light. Like the essence of Love itself. Tigger, the old Rhodesian Ridgeback, moseys in to check on things, to see what all the fuss is about. So handsome, so brave. He sees that all is well, shakes his noble head with fwapping ears, shakes all the way to the tips of his toes and long tail. Content with the scene, he turns to mosey back to the master bedroom, to lay in the morning sunlight on the giant bed. To breathe deeply. To dream of chasing lions, of conquering demons, and of protecting all whom he loves so dearly; that they may be safe, that they may love him also and always, in this dream.

> Pain will always have something to teach us, some glorious gift in its end.
> Breathe through it, stick with it.
> Like a birth—like the child. The most glorious gift, in the end.
> And with it—Bliss.

10:41 a.m.

Heart racing, sobbing again. Anzu lets out a big sigh, Ashaya is curled in my lap. I feel like I am back in something again, uncomfortable and I should not be alone, but I am. I am supposed to be the caretaker right now, I am supposed to drive through the wind to the animals who await my care. But I can barely hold my head up, deep stress breathing hot flash. I need to go lie down. My heart races. *Go lie down.* Is this normal? Am I okay? The dogs are watching me closely again.

12:06 p.m.

> Salt bath,
> (hot flash)
> so much sobbing, sadness, loss—
> baby, Momma, my baby—
> feels like I am so deeply in it again, and all alone.
> Dizzy, deep breaths.
> Anzu comes to me, licks my knee
> (these dogs are my support team).
> Strong wind out there, I will go out into it to
> tend Apollo at our house, and tend the old mare.
> Get 'er done and back here as soon as possible, my
> temporary home.
> Trees outside dancing, mountains stand sentinel.
> It's okay, baby,
> the humans do the best that they can,
> but remember still, you are not alone.
>
> Ooooh, boy,
> I did not know what I was getting myself into.
> I don't think Joan would have left town and been out of reach
> if she had known, either.
> It's okay, go home and get your hybrid—it will be easier to
> drive than the clutch truck.
> Shakey. Strong wind out there. Keep breathing. It's okay.

6:20 p.m.

> Definitely
> an Interesting
> day.

I got through it—good job, Laura!—basically on my own. It was closer to 4 p.m. when Brandi got my text messages and reached out to see if I was okay. When I texted that I was struggling and could not get a hold of Joan, she called within fifteen minutes, on her lunch break at the hospital. That was infinitely helpful, got me back in line. I was at my townhouse when she called, ended up laying on my bed for a while talking with her, with Anzu pressed to my side, Ashaya curled on my stomach, and Apollo curled down by my legs (he misses having us there, to be sure). Brandi said her initial Journey was not nearly as "emotional" as mine, but that in her therapy sessions following, a great deal of deeper emotion has been unveiling itself since then. She said she also has times when she feels as though she is back in it, which was a great relief for me to hear (when I was in the bathtub earlier, I felt FULL ON back in it, and it felt **super messed up** that Joan was not there to guide and take care of me). Brandi said she'd found herself crying in line at the grocery store yesterday. I felt so much less like a complete Crazy Person, talking with her. I felt like, yep, this is just what this looks like for me, and there is nothing to worry about. Just keep rolling with it, and flowing with this intense process as it unfolds.

She asked if I am finding that things I normally do without thinking are harder to navigate. I said, YES, like feeding the dogs or driving the car down a quiet country road, I find I have to focus intently on every little thing that I do. I told her I was laughing at myself yesterday as I drove out to the old mare's place, I felt as though I was in driver's ed, concentrating on every minute detail of the task. She said her counselor told her that for the next three or four weeks after a Journey our minds are "looser," that the old neuropathways aren't as predominant, so it's a great time to create new habits, to build new pathways. It will serve me, I believe, to take notes on what neuropathways I would like to strengthen at this time, this grand opportunity for rewiring.

After our conversation, it was much easier to recalibrate. Visiting with the old mare was good, and getting back to Tigger and the country homestead was even better. Made myself a good salad for supper, read more of this book, *How to Change Your Mind*. Got the dogs fed and walked them at sunset while a small herd of elk watched us from way across the forty-acre field (the dogs did not notice them, thankfully). I paused, facing the setting sun beyond the mountains, the trees, the elk. I closed my eyes, stood straight, hands in my warm pockets, and breathed. In. And out. Deeply, and slowly. I felt the soft touch of Light Momma on my brow, and the gentle words—*Oh, my darling, you are beautiful...* When I opened my eyes after what seemed to be a few minutes or more, all three dogs were near me—Ashaya to the right of me, and Tigger to my left, sniffing the breeze, apparently contemplating the sunset, as well. Anzu stood a few feet to Tigger's left, at the very same angle, doing the very same as we three. All aligned, taking in the sunset, sniffing the cool breeze.

In this moment, heaven.

Bliss.

Chapter 10
Right Where You're
Supposed to Be

"As a single footstep will not make a path on the earth,
so a single thought will not make a pathway in the mind.
To make a deep physical path, we walk again and again.
To make a deep mental path, we must think over and over
the kind of thoughts we wish to dominate our lives."

— Henry David Thoreau

A funny thing about my first Journey is that no one ever told me you actually have to do more than one. In fact, three intensive psychedelic sessions spaced four to six weeks apart are generally what's recommended for treating depression or PTSD, with plenty of regular ol' counseling sessions in between. When Joan mentioned this to me (*after* my first Journey), I did not find it funny at all. How had I not gathered this information earlier? You mean I had to go through all of that *again? Two more times?!*

In our pop-a-pill culture, this new-fangled treatment smacked of a magical cure for what ailed me, so I was ready to go through one journey and be *fixed*, by golly. Alas, this was going to be more work than I'd bargained for—this work of Doing the Fixing.

This notion of becoming "fixed" brings to mind an Imagine Dragons concert Wendy and I took the boys to a few years ago in Albuquerque, NM, where, to a crowd of 10,000 or so attentive fans, the lead singer, Dan Reynolds, spoke bravely, openly, of his own struggles with depression and suicidality. He concluded by declaring, "We are not broken—we do not need to be fixed."

Oh, how his words rang in me.

I just wanted to feel better, to feel happy more often than fleetingly, to feel **well** more often than not. I wanted to be able to live my life fully, to do good things for myself and for others. To not feel tugged upon by the undercurrents of fear and loneliness what seemed like most of the time.

I had much to process after that first Journey, and did so through my dreams, my journalings, and many long walks in the snowy woods with good dogs. I practiced listening to my body about what to eat (*not so much, not at night, and super, super clean*), and what to drink (*really ease up on the caffeine, my darling*), and when to sleep (*whenever you're sleepy, dear*). My mind became filled with nostalgia, and vivid dreams teeming with people from my past, with myriad lessons for the learning, if I could only see. I loved my friends' homestead where I was staying, though it nudged at an ache in me for a place in the country of my own.

I wrote, "I feel sadness and apprehension around knowing that the dogs and I will have to leave here in a couple of days, like being pulled away from a dream. I feel anxiety right now and a tightness in my chest, rising up into my throat, though I recognize it may partly be the delicious coffee kicking in. I remind myself that yesterday when I went to our townhouse to tend Apollo, it felt good to be there. Even the part where I walk in the front door and it still smells like Dad's house (I wonder what that smell could be?), I am reminded of slipping the key marked 'Dad' in the front doorknob, when the house was still his, when he was inside, sick with the cancer. I remember his smiley-face notes taped to the front door, reading, 'Ring the Doorbell and Come In.' I remember him sitting at his table by the big window looking out toward the mountains, or finding him sleeping in his room. He was so lonely, and also joyful at times, like when I'd first come in the front door...

Ah, this thing of life. 'Tis a mixed bag, for sure.

I have homestead on the brain now. Wisconsin, Goat Farm, all of that. I do so wonder what the future holds."

* * * * * *

Wednesday, March 10, 2021
Maybe it is 6:30 a.m.

A fresh layer of snow this morning, a light sugar-powder dusting over everything. Beautiful. The wind howling, swirling. I was awake for some time in the night—this seems to be the pattern, to sleep well for some time, then awaken between the two cycles of shallow sleep and REM, so important for the emotional processing through dreams. This is when I suffer night sweats, this is when I toss and turn and slide through consciousness in fits and starts. This is when I chase sleep like a shimmering unicorn through a magical forest—elusive, at best.

"Be gentle with yourself," Joan had said about this time after the Journey. And how long does this time last? Three or four weeks? "Be gentle with yourself" seems to have become one of those cliché catch-phrases, or maybe that's just how it feels right now to the cynical part in me, my "Protector," who has begun raising its angry head again in the past couple of days. It has no patience for this woo-woo, touchy-feely bullshit. It wants ACTION, it wants SOLUTIONS, it wants CONTROL of this weakness and these awful, uncomfortable feelings, NOW. For fuck's sake.

Perhaps it is the Universe reminding me that these hard parts can be gotten through, there is no need to resist them, or react, or try to fight them off. In the struggle, the snare tightens—let loose, relax and breathe into it—it's okay, it's okay, it's okay. Like a zebra caught in the clutches of a lion, struggling for its life with all the power and force of adrenaline—it wants to live. But then, at a certain point...it lets go, it concedes. It surrenders its body to the lion's jaws; it lets its body go, that the lion and its pride may feed.

I am processing a whole lot of grief right now. I will do well to remember to cut myself some slack for that, to give myself some space.

After my delicious, big cup of coffee has been drunk, and I fix myself a cup of yerba maté, by the kitchen sink, I have a vision, a feeling in my chest that I've had before—of a sweet little house with tall windows, surrounded by sunlight, nature, and trees. Where the sky is huge, and glorious at night, where I can stand with head tilted toward the heavens to see all the stars...like here, like this place. Like the goat farm in Wisconsin. Like someplace else, just for me. Where my mornings begin with yoga and meditation, then outside into the rising sunlight. Tending chickens, throwing hay to llamas, and a couple of horses, maybe. Where a Guardian dog joins me dutifully on my rounds, smiling, tail wagging, harkening back to my days with Govinda the Elder. A couple of goats, for packing, and for milk. Gardens, composting, a pond designed and built by Fisher, with Koi, and other fish of his choosing. After first chores and time outside catching the rising sunlight, back indoors for breakfast, and to write...until I don't feel like writing anymore. Then a hike with the llamas, goats nibbling along our path, and galloping free with the dogs. A couple of hours, then pausing for a light lunch. Afternoons spent tending the homestead, fences, pastures, beautiful spaces, gardening, building artful structures and things. On windy or rainy days inside, reading, writing, painting animal portraits and scenes. Wood stove, lovely music, creatures gathered 'round, dozing contentedly. Writing letters to faraway friends. Evenings of chores and walks again, of simple, delicious, home-made food. Of gratitude, and contemplation. Claw-foot bathtub, fire crackling in the woodstove. Climbing into bed when the sun goes down, sighing by candlelight. Peaceful, harmonious living among all creatures of our family, and surrounding. This is my vision, my dream.

I wonder where it will be.

Thursday, March 11, 2021
6:28 a.m.

Met with Joan briefly yesterday morning while the dogs waited patiently in the truck. Told her about my anxiety, about worrying what will happen when Fisher comes home after his two weeks at his father's, because I'm feeling so vulnerable and raw. Told her I've had moments when I feel like this is just stupid, and bullshit, that I'm feeling even worse than I did before the Intensive a week ago, so what the fuck? She sat calmly in her comfy chair, smiling gently, sipping her tea. Yes, she said, yep this is all normal. You're doing great, she said. You are right where you're supposed to be. Words poured out of me, and it all felt like so much to process. She agreed that, yes—it's a lot. She told me I am really sensitive, that the medicine worked really well on me. I told Joan the story of Wendy and her friend coming to my apartment when they were tripping on acid, and Wendy telling her friend that I am "like this all the time."

It feels as though I am always so close to some "other reality," I said to Joan. So easily I can be pulled through the thin gossamer of perception to inhabit this other realm, which most people seem largely unaware of, except perhaps in dreams. A reality which most people do not choose to feel, or see. So, I end up feeling like the Crazy Person in this realm, as though I don't belong here, I don't fit in with the status quo. I am "too sensitive," I was told in my youth, and the message is still received.

But, too sensitive for what? For whom?

"You've got to toughen up, girl. You're a smart cookie, you'll figure it out," judging voices have said in my mind and memory.
Ah, yes. All of that.
Well, I suppose what I've figured out, y'all, is that there IS another way—
Welcome to my world—ha-ha—leave your bullshit at the door.

Look at those mountains bathed in the morning sunlight, the delicate clouds lingering 'round their peaks. See not only with your eyes, but *feel it* in your chest. FEEL that beauty, awe, and respect coursing through every vein in you. Breathe it in, slowly, deeply—*feel it.*

Now, exhale.

See our little rabbit friend hopping around outside the back of this house, how peacefully it forages for its morning sustenance. Feel how soft its fur would be to the touch, feel how its little heart beats so quickly. Feel its tiny, quick, rabbit's breath. How exquisite, all of this! A feast for all senses, in every moment, with every breath. My God—my Gods—to the Divine within and surrounding us, to the Force which connects us all (Yoda spoke the truth, by golly!). The dogs sighing in the bedroom, the birds tittering outside in the trees. All of this. ALL of it, and also,

so
much
more...

* * * * * *

"All roads lead to Andrew Huberman," in the words of Rich Roll, plant-based ultra-marathoner, author, and podcaster extraordinaire. Feeling anxious, getting to practice breathing techniques learned from the Huberman Lab Podcast. Deep inhale through the nose, then deeper still, then long exhale...Relax.

We are on the path. Just as all roads of insight lead to Andrew Huberman, all roads of my heart lead me Home, wherever that may be—what feels right and loving for me, surrounded by animals, and peace, and space, and trees.

Relax, Laura. Just relax.

* * * * * *

Wednesday, March 17, 2021
Sometime after 5 a.m.

I was having strange dreams about puppets on strings, and lots of cows, and mud, and blood in the snow. I was making plans to buy two plots of land, old farms, and thinking, well, then the animals will be safe. I was wearing a long, old-fashioned dress, and trying to squeeze through some sort of metal chicken-chute door. I was concerned about getting hurt, but was following an elderly woman wearing another such dress, and she was doing just fine, didn't seem concerned at all. Maybe the elderly woman was supposed to be my dear friend, Dolores, in Wisconsin, but she didn't look like her at all.

I had been sleeping ten or more hours a night at Tigger's homestead, especially after the MDMA session. Nothing like that now that I'm back home with Fisher, he will not allow it. Last night I was in bed by 8 p.m., exhausted, fell asleep with one hand on Ashaya to my left, the other with fingers buried in Anzu's scruff to my right. I was awoken by Fisher turning on the bathroom light outside my bedroom door, getting ready for bed. I got frustrated when he turned on the lights a second time, then blustered into my room to get Ashaya. He does not understand that I need to get a good night's sleep (already challenged by waking up at all hours of the night with hot flashes and night sweats), or else I am not functional. It does not hit home to him that I am trying really, REALLY hard just to take good care of myself so I can be a better parent for him, as much as anything else, rather than some ragey, out-of-whack Momster. If he won't let me take care of myself, then what is the point? When it turns into these battles, these power-struggles between us. He obviously does not see the correlation at all, as a teenager concerned mainly with the whim of every moment. While I, as his mother, do the best that I can with what flawed and incomplete mothering tools I possess in my befuddling "Life as a Human on this Planet" toolbox…and where are the instructions for this fucking thing, anyway? I am doing the very best that I can with what I have been given, as well as with what I'm learning as I go.

Fisher tells me he feels like he's paying for my "shitty childhood." He tells me I've got shit on my boots that gets scraped off on him, and he's just going to end up scraping it off on someone else down the road.

I don't really know what to say to that, astute observation that it is. What is the solution? To learn how to clean off both our respective pairs of boots? To kick our fucking boots off altogether, and learn how to frolic carefree in the grass?

I don't know.
Maybe so.

All I know is that moment by moment, bit by bit, we are both doing the best we can. Sometimes that may not look so great.

I was always afraid I would be a terrible mother; that I was too socially awkward, reclusive, emotionally all over the board, easily overwhelmed and overstimulated. I remember an older friend (a mother figure, at the time) telling me in my mid-twenties that I would make a good mom because I was so good at taking care of animals. But animals are intensely forgiving; they will wait around for you to feed and play with them at about the times they're used to, judging by where the sun is in the sky. They could really care less what time you get there to muck out the barn, or if you're feeling melancholy or downright depressed, or if you haven't showered or washed your hair for days. They don't care. They don't blame you or tell you what an awful mom you are. They don't look at you sideways when they're out of clean pants, even though they have not explored the full dryer, expecting pants only to appear magically folded in their drawer.

I do not know what to Do here. I do not know what to Be. Part of me wants to just go back to the goat farm in Wisconsin, to milk goats and make soap, and hang-out with Dolores in her bountiful garden. She could teach me about canning, and how to bake her exquisite bread, until she decides to finally give up the ghost (a hundred or so years being quite enough of all this), and leave our earthly realm.

My beloved child, whom I cherish in a way more profound than any other being I could imagine loving. Sometimes I don't even know how to *be* with him, how to take care of him, I don't know what he needs—truly NEEDS. I feel so deeply saddened in my heart. I feel like there are weights tethered to my limbs, laying upon my chest. I am not sure how to set myself free.

Thursday, April 1, 2021
6:05 a.m.

With all roads leading to Andrew Huberman, yesterday evening washing dishes after supper with Fisher while he prepared rice pudding for dessert, I listened to an interview in which Andrew spoke of circadian rhythms, and how it's important to set everything else aside to seize the ninety minutes in which one's creativity is honed, to be expressed with its fullest potential—whatever that looks like for you, and whatever time of day that becomes present for you. I heard his remark and thought, Aw, heck yeah! For me, it is the writing before sunrise, that is the time of my flow. When the words come trickling out of me like spring water from deep within, growing steadily, sometimes into a gushing torrent...Yes. Thank you, Dr. Huberman. Validation feels divine.

I suppose this is why I feel such conflict with Fisher in the evenings, when he wants to stay up sorting through his Magic cards or working on projects, and I feel desperate to get to bed. To get my rest, so I can rise early and invigorated, make my coffee before sunrise, and sit with my journal and my words while the rest of the house still sleeps. Last night he and I reached an agreement that he would close his bedroom door to keep his bedside lamp light from pouring into my room (I keep my door open so the cat can come and go as he pleases), and he would promise to turn his light out at nine. I guess that worked out pretty well, though I do worry about him losing track of time, and not getting enough sleep, himself.

Right now I feel a little anxious in my chest and throat, a tightness growing as the sun begins to rise, because I am running out of this time to myself, despite waking up (no alarm) at five. Hmm. No ninety minutes of creativity for me this morning, Dr. Huberman. Admittedly, I laid in bed for quite a while this morning, knees drawn to my chest beneath the blankets, hugging them firmly, giving my hips and back a nice stretch. I thought about the feel of Beorn's muscles beneath his thin, well-worn tee-shirt yesterday, when we met to discuss him putting dog-proof screens in my truck's topper. His shirt fit his frame perfectly, and smelled suspiciously clean for a man who said he'd been working on a car half the day—had he changed his shirt before I got there? Or does this man just never sweat? Knees to my chest, I thought of the slight awkwardness between us, how my words were coming in unsure little jumps and starts. I wondered at his silences, at his sometimes abruptness, wondered if it was just because he feels awkward and insecure, too. If these are just our Protectors rising to greet one another, to suss each other out in a curious little dance. Circling like big cats, wondering if it's safe to draw near. And is it safe to draw near? Then, unexpectedly, he opened his strong arms, drawing me in, enfolding and engulfing me against his muscley chest.

Sweet Jesus, how it feels to be held.

Out by the back of my pickup truck, feeling self-conscious about my extra Covid layer of thickness wriggled into form-fitting clothes, his arms around me silently, just holding me. I found myself thinking quietly out loud, "I should let myself just do this, just be here…" because being held is such a precious gift, especially now, in times of social distancing. To be held in such a way by a full-grown human, and all. To be held by this beautiful man. I was aware that it felt hard for me to stay there, to keep myself from pulling away. That some part of me wanted it so badly, hence, making it unsafe. It felt to me as though he was fully present; still, and strong. As though giving himself fully to the embrace, while I grappled with my own inner conflicts, trying to find that stillness, that surrender—that *presence* in his arms. I tried to allow myself to breathe in the smell of him, to allow for the soft bliss of feeling his warm neck against my lips.

This does not feel real to me—it feels too perfect, too beautiful, too divine. This work of art in flesh and blood and bone, with his own awkwardness and long pauses, his own hesitations—holding me. What is going on in that mind? As we let go and stumble around each other like bumbling, precious puppies. As I can't stop touching him (is that okay?), as our hands and bodies seem drawn to one another again and again. As we sit for a while with his legs dangling from the tailgate, with my knees around him from inside the bed of my truck. We talked a little (what did we even talk about? This and that) while I worked on his amazing back, pressing my thumbs and knuckles into his muscles, squeezing his shoulders and arms with my long fingers and hands, strong from decades of cleaning horse stalls.

Ah, yes—this. This touch, this nurturing. This is where I find myself grounding, coming into my balance, at last. It reminded me of that time in Minneapolis in 2001, sitting across from Henry on a tour bus after an intense Rollins Band show. To this day I'm not sure why he invited me onto the bus (unlike the next time in Madison, when it was bitterly cold. Turning to the tour bus that time, he sighed with resignation. *"Come on,"* he said, and I followed him like a pup. After humoring me for as long as he was willing to tolerate, I was to get a stern talking to. "It's not you," he said finally, "I just don't date."). He certainly never gave any indication of wanting to get in my pants, or anything unseemly of the sort. I believe he was just being gracious to this starry-eyed gal who wanted nothing more than to be in his presence a while longer. I've long observed Henry to be gracious, while also taking no shit. After Rolando first brought me to a spoken word show at Seventh Street Entry in Minneapolis in 1988, I saw Henry speak several more times over as many years, and I devoured most of his books.

Seated across the narrow tour bus aisle from him, I asked Henry questions now and then, but mostly I listened to him tell stories—my own private show—noticing that he wouldn't look at me directly. From the corner of my eye, I could see his gaze turn to me only when I looked away. After some time of this, I asked if he wanted a back rub. He shot me a quizzical glance, and I quickly clarified, "No, not like that—I mean, I just watched you basically kick your own ass for two and a half hours onstage." I ventured, "You could probably use a back rub."

Henry agreed. He nestled in on the floor with his back to me, muscular shoulders between my knees, and the awkwardness subsided instantly. He no longer had to fill space with words, he did not have to avoid looking at me. My hands could do what comes naturally to them; to caress, to knead, to soothe. I found my center, my grounding, through working his strong neck, his shoulders, his tattooed back, and arms. I marveled at how even Henry Rollins is just flesh and bone beneath all his intensity, his sternness, his sweat. Beneath all those powerful words.

Like Beorn now to my touch, a glorious and guarded little boy in the body of this grown man—who worries, works his fingers to the bone, yet can hold me in the most firmly gentle embrace. As I drove away from him that day, I licked my lips, tasting salt from his skin.

Ah, yes, he *does* sweat.

Sunday, April 4, 2021
6:27 a.m.

Thinking about those pat-pat hugs some people give, not a *real* hug like those of Beorn. The real hugs that he gives, but then takes away again—poof!—just like that, into the ether he goes.

Humans are scary.

It feels safer to be alone, and yet, I get so lonely. I don't know what to do with these feelings; I want to purge them, or make peace with them, or just fucking *something.* Something. I don't know.

It was interesting when a girlfriend from the big city observed what a solitary lifestyle I lead; how I don't have People around me all day long, just the animals, mostly. When she asked if I get lonesome, my answer didn't feel quite accurate—that I don't, because I am so focused on the animals, on connecting with them, and *being* with them. This is a true statement, most certainly, and also—I do crave human company. Not in the way of desiring someone by my side every hour of every day, but in proximity, my goodness, yes, that would be lovely. I imagine what it might be like to have a partner—an equal—to come home to. Someone with whom to feel deeply connected, by our mutual choosing. Someone I may hold in my heart so fondly as both lover and true friend. For all our similarities, and all of our differences, too, to have each other's backs through life, until the very end. Yes, please, Universe—please send that human being to me. Let me know it in my chest, and by the glimmer in his eye when he has arrived. Yes, please, let me feel strong and beautiful in his presence, and feel safe in my moments of vulnerability—to feel always supported, never weak.

I do not feel that this is too much for me to ask. I feel as though something in my own energy has been blocking this connection I desire, has been blocking it my whole life. I do not know the answer to this riddle, and sometimes worry that I am running out of time…to build a little home in the country with this someone, to have our little family, our garden, and chickens plucking around in the yard. What a glorious vision, yet here I am over fifty, my heart still feeling the passions of my youth, and in this curious emotional holding pattern—or not even. I'm not sure exactly what it is, or what I should do. Am I fulfilling what I desire for myself in this glorious life I've been granted? Among these mountains that John Denver's voice sang to me of when I was a little girl, with these dogs and the cat, and the most beautiful, magical man-cub asleep in his bedroom upstairs, old Chihuahua close by his side. This must be the dream I have created, that I am creating. This must be some version (unmistakably) of *my* dream.

Monday, April 5, 2021
5:10 a.m.

Yesterday marked the four-week anniversary of my MDMA session, and man, it was a motherfucker. In the past few weeks, I have had moments of feeling incredibly grateful for the insights born of that chemical opening, and also, several times I have questioned the wisdom of inducing such a dramatic shift in my very sensitive internal ecosystem. I already feel that I am swayed by the mercies of the wind—does this intensive dismantling of my inner emotional structure truly serve me, or ultimately just break me down? And how, oh, how, do I build myself up again?

Is this truly where I'm supposed to be?

All of this intensity. All of this fear I find myself grappling with. Yesterday felt as bad as it has been, spanning from tears and feelings of hopelessness, helplessness, to quick bursts of frustrated rage. When little Manu jumped up on me, scratching my leg. When I could not find the keys to the hybrid and Fisher snarked at me that we were late, we should just take the truck. When Fisher was downstairs not answering me as I called out to him from my room. "You were mumbling, I couldn't hear you," he said, but I suspect the truth was more that he did not want to come to me, to be near me in my tearful state, laying like some sickly monster version of Mom in bed. *I* don't want to be near me like this, so how could I possibly blame him? I only wish to get away from myself, from the weakness, from the pain.

I had images in my mind from in my early twenties, when I lived in Arizona. I had a sort of friend (though what were we, really? I don't remember us being full-on lovers, so I suppose that made us friends) who had a colorful, somewhat dangerous lifestyle, but a simple, soothing demeanor. I entered his fancy apartment early one morning to find him asleep with a very pretty, mostly naked young woman in his bed. For whatever reason, it seemed reasonable for me to climb right in there with them, curled on the other side of my friend. The young woman seemed understandably displeased; without a word, she slid from beneath the sheets and left. I stayed for the better part of the day, right there in my friend's bed.

I don't know why that image came to my mind yesterday, as I lay sobbing and writhing and missing my mother desperately. When Fisher rode his bike to a friend's house (understandably, and for the best) and Anzu would not be near me. When I could not stop sobbing, wanting to claw my way out of my own skin. What fuckery is this? Who the fuck wants this? When I'd spent the morning texting with Beorn until he dropped out again; too much, maybe, for him. I had begun only by saying that I would figure the topper thing out on my own, and thank you for offering, but it seemed as though he already had too much on his plate. He replied, texting, oh, no—he's just sitting on his porch enjoying a cup of coffee, and he already ordered the supplies for the topper windows, they would be there Tuesday, and what happened? Why the change? Is there a rush? Could I explain? So, I did. I let the walls I'd erected with my first vague message tumble down. I explained the triggers from the past few days, of all our "miscommunications," and having to drop by his house without confirming (we'd had tentative plans about the topper, but then he didn't answer his phone), to feeling dumb and frustrated with myself for being afraid of his Pitbull who trotted out back to see who was visiting—how was I to know what a sweetheart she was? He had a reason for each of the things I brought up, from his phone glitching-out, to missing social cues. "I'm not too far off the spectrum," he confided, which I felt grateful to read, because that makes perfect sense to me.

When I felt we were actually in a conversation (albeit by text-message), I began to open up, feeling some relief at the connection, the exploration, at the insights we were perhaps coming to. I told him I'm very selective with the human company I keep, and about being socially awkward, and limiting my social interactions. He said he can relate, that he is socially awkward, too, that he keeps himself well-guarded. I professed that I would like for him to let his guard down with me.

Then he was gone.

No more replies, no, "Hey, I've got to boogie," or anything. Maybe he'd finished his cup of coffee and decided he was done texting about all these *feelings* for the day. Maybe it was simply time to put those guards back up and move on. After that, it was just me emoting into the wind, with no reply at all from Beorn. After that, it was just me sobbing in my bed alone, feeling useless, and helpless, wanting to cease to exist…but, no.

Oh, no.

I could not leave my darling child—my God, my Gods, oh, my Goddess divine—I cannot do that, even when he can't stand to be near me. I cannot do that to these creatures who depend on me. I cannot do that to those who love me. I very simply cannot.

I just have to get through it, I just have to survive. I just have to keep living, and get my bearings, and be solid for those who depend on me to live. I just have to pull my shit together—that is the only thing to do.

It is interesting that the imagery in my mind, as I lay miserable in bed, was of a time where I surrendered completely. Where I put myself in someone else's hands, worthy of my submission or not (it may have been mere folly for my friend, as I climbed boldly between his sheets). Where I allowed myself to be handcuffed to the bed, allowed him to keep me there for the day. I was in his charge, in his care. The burdens of my own decision-making deferred to a pretty fellow, who was pretty messed-up, as well. But he was ultimately kind, and sweet to me, and he was good at taking charge of things. He relieved me of my responsibilities for the day, kept me as his pet for that short while. He took care of me, and I welcomed it, gratefully, even though it meant being chained.

Geeze, Louise.

Thirty years down the road from then, where I am now a mother, a homeowner, a business owner. Where I still struggle sometimes just to figure out my own needs, and how to get them met. When my heart still longs to be cared for, to be understood, to allow my own guards to come down, to just feel SAFE—I am still not sure what it means to be safe. I still long for that security, that sanctuary, that peace, when I don't even know what it means, really. If it's possible, if it's real. How to find it, if it is.

Upstairs, Fisher's alarm goes off, playing music of the Shire, from *The Lord of the Rings*, and, oh—that we could live in such a place.

Chapter 11
The Muck

"It's gonna get messy before it gets clean."

— Tim Ferris, in conversation with Brené Brown

Tuesday, April 6, 2021
4:45 a.m.

I remember climbing into bed around 9 p.m. after not feeling like taking a shower, and my sheets are overdue for a change anyway, so who cares about a little leftover sweat and barn dust from hiking with Brandi in the morning, cleaning stalls in the afternoon. I feel all discombobulated, anyway, haven't even been making my bed. Anzu goes upstairs during the day and sleeps on my exposed sheets and pillows, shedding on them with her undercoat now coming out in celebratory tufts for spring. She is glorious, and all parts of her are welcome (as the saying goes) in my eyes, even her soft undercoat of bunny-like hairs. Besides, it's my fault if I'm not making my bed. It's my fault if I'm allowing myself to roll with this state of feeling all whack-a-doodle, of flopping around like a fish out of water, not allowing myself to just get my bearings and drag myself by my fins back to sea. I can blame menopause and these freaking hot flashes. I can blame childhood trauma, or that stupid lady who handed her biting dog over to me. I can blame my hyper-sensitivity to EVERYTHING, ALWAYS. I can blame no longer living in the countryside, missing those owls out in the forest and the deer in my yard. I can blame the noisy vehicles that I hear now outside my townhouse. I can blame being surrounded by too much humanity.

None of that is helpful, really. None of that will get me to where I'd like to be, in the end.

And where would I like to be, really? I mean right here, right now.

I'd like to be right where I am. Sitting at my mother's antique table, the one I understand she sanded and finished by hand. In this townhouse that my dad had built to his refined specifications, after moving here from Wisconsin, after his divorce, and wanting to be near his girls. He inhabited this townhome proudly for the few years before he died. I'd like to be present with the sounds of water trickling from the filter in my son's beloved aquarium. My belly full of coffee and goat milk. Shelves full of so many books that would be helpful, no doubt, to read. Clients wanting to book pet care already for the summertime, and plans of my own blossoming, for a drive to the Midwest with my glorious teenaged son. Life continues to unfold, curiously, beautifully, weirdly. The strangest mystery. The unraveling of the greatest ball of yarn.

I know what I ought to do, intellectually, to take care of my body and my soul. I have all the knowledge, I have so many tools, and new insights pouring in on me daily.

At the closing of our hike yesterday, Brandi asked about the qualities I seek in my friendships, and in a romantic relationship. I know she questions my choice to continue interactions with Beorn despite his elusiveness, his unpredictability, his seeming inability to follow through in ways I would like him to. He has his own ways of going about things, that's for stinkin' sure, like the day he pulled over on the highway on his way to the dump, read my wordy messages about wanting him to let me in...He replied, explaining the scenario, saying he was giving me his whole-heart answer beside the road. "This is me letting you in."

Brandi asked why I don't date men older than me, who might offer more stability.

It makes me think of the eighteen years between myself and Bear (who had been so wonderfully into loving me, and he, the younger one), and how, at the time, I became acutely aware of that same eighteen years between my dad and his then wife. How she teasingly called my dad "old man," which made me cringe every time. It became a cautionary tale, though I'm sure there must have been challenges besides their age difference; they eventually divorced, spurring my Dad to move to Colorado to "be near his daughters" after more than a decade away from us, and for what became the last years of his life.

I look at Beorn and see him in his prime, though he sometimes laments feeling "old," which makes me wary of the romantic draw between us. Though our nine-year difference is not far off from many of my significant romantic relationships, as I season with age, the span feels more pronounced. If what I desire in my heart of hearts is truly a Life Partner, rather than just a Lover for Now (something I've never been good at. Loving the feeling of falling in love, I will always get attached)…Well, then, I would be wise to stick to prospects closer to my own age.

But, who knows. Women tend to live longer, anyway.

Also worthy of considering: There seem to be so few souls to begin with, who I am drawn to in such a way. Perhaps if Beorn and I were to become lovers even for a shortish while, that could be worthy of exploration….

Take it easy, now, little girl. One day at a time.

Wednesday, April 7, 2021
5:56 a.m.

My counseling session yesterday morning was hard. It is so difficult for me to stay connected with all these uncomfortable feelings; with the anger and frustration, with all the insecurities, the doubt, the shame, the fear. Isn't this why I did the freaking Hoffman Process? Though it seems now that the Process was just a taste, merely an opening of a door for me to walk through, to a new realm of possibility, supported by lovely humans and eating delicious food along that way. Still, there are all the old patterns and inclinations which cling to me, these old ways of being and feeling, of stepping gingerly and fearfully through life. There are all these things which tug at me, constantly—these apprehensions, these doubts. I found myself sobbing for just a moment in Joan's presence, then collecting myself again...she says to stay with that feeling, of wanting to just not feel this way—but, noh. Protector steps in, says, *Oh, boy, that's quite enough, now.*

Gotta pull it together, gotta keep it together. Gotta be strong, and gotta do it on your own, baby.

I had an insight, an impression, of Ashaya as Little Baby Girl (as from my Journey, realizing she is just like me)—and part of me wants to protect her, to keep her safe. Another part of me gets frustrated with her, gets annoyed and angry when she needs "too much," when she is too rukkussy or doesn't mind my commands or is licking her bum in my bed—so gross! I feel anger toward her, then I feel angry at myself for not being kinder and more patient with her, for being a terrible mother. Just like with Fisher; I get upset with him, then angry with myself for being a terrible mother.

And where was my mother? Why did she leave me and never come home? Was it because there was something wrong with me? The little girl part of me wonders. Or was it because she was not a good mother? Even the thought feels like blasphemy.

Obviously, I know it was not my mother's fault that she died. I know she would have wanted to be there for her babies, and for her soulmate, my father. Obviously, it was not her fault, and still...as a little girl, just three years old, how was I to know? I did not understand. I remember being on the stairs in our old house on Bagley Parkway, in Madison. I remember my dad being angry with me, and me feeling frightened and sad. I asked him when Mommy was coming home. I remember him turning away from me, softening a bit to tell me, she is not coming home, that Mommy has died. I didn't know what that meant, what it meant...that Mommy had gone away forever.

I don't remember what happened next, but I remember feeling confused, and alone. The feelings which have informed my life. The feelings which set my stage.

It is no wonder I am compulsively drawn to a man like Beorn—Jesus, he is so much like my father. Strong, tall, and handsome to the eye. Wanting to prove himself, to be valued and of service to others. Then there is his underbelly, simultaneously guarded and wanting to be known; the ever-present push-me/pull-you. The kindness coupled with distance, self-doubt, elusiveness. Beorn confided once that he's always hardest on himself. It makes perfect sense and seems crystal clear to me this morning, that the little girl on the stairs who feels sad and alone, who wants her mommy to come home, she also wants her daddy to protect her, something he's unable to do in his own state of grief and despair. He is just trying to survive the loss of his wife—the love of his life. He is trying to get through his pain, too. So, the little girl grows up feeling frightened and alone, disconnected from a world which seems scary and unavailable to her. The daddy who lashes out in his pain and rage, who frightens and hurts the little girl. It makes sense that, trying to right those wrongs, she grows into a woman who is drawn to an elusive man, a single father who represents his daughter's noble Protector. He also represents the man-child who himself needs loving and nurturing. Yes, indeed, that makes perfect sense to me, psychologically. It also makes sense to my heart.

Then to step back and recognize, Beorn is not the father figure I can repair my childhood through. He is not my fantasy lover/partner who can heal those wounds and magically make me whole. He is his own glorious and complicated version of his own wounded little boy self, grown into this man who is making his way in the world. Who, like me, and like everyone else, is just doing the best that he can.

Monday, April 12, 2021
6:35 a.m. or so

I am so grateful for my little weekend trip to Santa Fe with Wendy, to explore some culture and museums. To hear the Native American drummers in the downtown park, to watch the hoop dancers, and to buy their CD called "Lightening Boy," after the dancer's young nephew who had died. To watch all the humans doing their various human things, whether or not these things resonated with me. To enter the Georgia O' Keefe Museum and feel immediately awash with emotion, nearly brought to tears. *These are her actual paintings*, I thought. *These are the actual images born of her paint brushes, held by her hands.* All my life I have seen these images, as an artist my Nana deeply admired. This woman I have been so curious about since I first began learning of her in earnest when I attended the alternative high school, Malcom Shabazz. When I first began to feel as though she could be something of a role model for me, for so little of her that I knew. And now, all these years later, in the presence of her actual work—I was amazed. I was in awe. I was deeply moved, to say the least.

Remember this feeling. Let this inspiration linger profoundly, let it ring true, and help to motivate me throughout my days, with Life so fleeting and precious. I do not wish to waste a single moment of it, bogged in the mire of fear or depression or malaise. Please, please, please help me seize every gifted moment of the profound glory of the rising sun, of the birds who must be out there singing in those trees across the rocky field, even if right now I can't hear them. All these precious gifts lain before me by the Universe in every moment, please, oh, please let me recognize them and be grateful, let me be glad. Let me embrace this inspiration, this motivation, this opportunity to live a full and open-hearted Life that I choose, of Creativity, Purpose, and Light.

Please, please help me—Spirits, Creators, Angels, Guides—ALL who are present in the Now and always Forever. Please stay with me, support me in my quest, in my ongoing Journey. Please guide me in my striving to lead a full and Good life.

Thank you.

What a gift this all is, truly.
    And truly I am grateful
        for the reminders,
           for the guides.

Wednesday, May 5, 2021

What I posted on Facebook the other day, after being on it for far too long:

"Never going to be one of those make-up girls.
Never going to get my legs (or any other bits of me) waxed.
Always going to have a little horse or goat grime under my
    fingernails.
Always going to have dog-nose prints Jackson Pollacked on
    my windows, and fur on everything I own.
Never going to know just what to wear, or what to say to
    be polite.
Going to feel self-conscious about carrying an extra few
    pounds, but still overindulge when I'm lonely and alone.
Going to cry when I mean it, going to laugh too loud
    sometimes.
Going to curse inappropriately on occasion, without realizing.
Going to run a bit late, most of the time.
Going to get scared, or angry, or insecure.
Going to get heady, or wordy, or dig too deep, or push too far.
Going to love too hard sometimes, I tell you what.
Going to growl like an animal when I'm pissed-off.
Going to act like a total dork, and make dumb jokes, too.
Going to fall on the floor, rolling, kicking, and clutching my
    sides because I'm laughing so freaking hard.

Never going to apologize for who I am, or who I strive to
become.
Love me like that, I tell you now, or let me bless you, and
send you on your way."

Monday, May 10, 2021
4:44 a.m.

The cat purring behind me on the guest bed. The U2
song "All I Want Is You" playing along in my head to the montage
scene in the film *Reality Bites* (so emotional! If you don't know
what I mean, go watch the film.) And, oh, my goodness—falling
asleep last night with so many images in my mind, with my lips
red and swollen from passionate kisses, with my limbs stretched
and sore from good use. Though my stretchy pants stayed decidedly in place, if there was any question as to whether Beorn and
I would be, *could be*, physically (sexually) compatible, the answer
is a resounding *Hails, Yes*.

Our strengths and our submissions, our gives and our takes.
The way we moved together so easily, the way our mouths, our
legs, our hips fit together perfectly. My God, it feels as though
it's been forever since I've experienced that with someone, in
an honest and connected way. It has been years, for certain,
since I have felt the gentle exploration of innocence rise into a
straining, heavy-breathed devouring of true passion, of desire.
Something which rises not from the primal urge to fuck, or to
procreate—something which rises from the very core of the
Earth, through our bodies and our souls...Longing to connect,
to trust, to express in its most truthful and explosive terms—
LOVE. To give that, and to receive it. To stay present in that
essence with another being of flesh and blood, rather than to
be pulled away by fear.

At least, that is how it felt for me.

And it felt good. This—our first solid exploration of connection, of vulnerability, of trust. It felt good, and comfortable,

and easy. I was able to nurture him, and he was able to receive, gratefully. I played Iron and Wine on the little boombox in my room, feeling comfortable singing along softly with the words as I worked his beautiful muscles and bones. It felt so simple, so fulfilling to me, that blessed touch. Me in my power. Home.

Later, lying on our bare backs with legs entangled, I declared to him outright, with a soft smile, "I have a hard time trusting people—"

"Me, too," he replied quickly.

"Well, maybe we can learn to trust each other," I said, knowing full well that such a thing requires experience, and time.

What a very interesting Mother's Day.

Another interesting thing earlier, while trying to consciously let go of my attachment to Beorn's arrival (he had been ambiguous about what time, stating other commitments that had to be fulfilled first), I sat myself down on the landing of the stairs, facing the bookshelves. I was drawn to the book *Mastery of Love* by Don Miguel Ruiz, and opened it randomly to Chapter Two, "The Loss of Innocence." It spoke of how when you're a young child you are full of Love and Joy, expressing it through exuberant connection and play. Sometimes our mothers or fathers punish us for being too energetic or excitable, so we begin to lose our Trust. We don't understand why we are being punished for the joyous expressions which flow so freely from us.

I was thinking about the whole mother, father, trust thing. Thinking about why it is such an intense trigger for me to feel as though I'm waiting on a man who I'm not convinced is going to show up, then feeling utterly wrecked when he doesn't (a recurring theme for me with Beorn). After reading for a little while, I decided to lay on the sofa and listen to a guided transcendental meditation, which has no words, only sound. I ended up having a vision, or a dream, of sorts. It was as though I was being born...I could hear my mother's heartbeat all around me, I was surrounded by safety and warmth.

I was being guided toward a light, then I was emerging from the nurturing warmth of her body...then the images became blurred, and she was gone.

Shift to an image of being in our house at Bagley Parkway at night, and Daddy was away on a date. My sisters and I were supposed to be sleeping, but I carried my giant stuffed Snoopy dog to my dad's bedroom and climbed into his bed, where I fell asleep while waiting for him to come home.

I remember the first time, he carried me back to my own little bed, I remember him tucking me in. But after that first time, if he found me asleep in his bed, he made me walk back to my room by myself. I felt abandoned, betrayed, and stopped going to his room on the nights he was away. I had forgotten all about that, but in remembering through the dream, I knew it was true. The feelings of it were true.

On the sofa back in present time, I wept, tears streaming down my face. I felt anxious, then, though the relaxing sound meditation in my headphones played on. I reached over to the coffee table, looked through bleary eyes at my phone—there was a message from Beorn, asking if it was okay to head over now. I wiped away my tears, collected myself, and texted in reply, "Yes."

Chapter 12
Curiosity,
or
Journey Number Two

"Curiosity is really the super-power for the second half of our lives."

— Brené Brown, talking with Tim Ferriss

Friday, May 14, 2021
Just before sunrise, pinks and blues in the sky.

Journey day, so no coffee for me this morning. Tea, with a little coconut cream in it, and I'll have strawberries and some banana in a bit. Last night I folded laundry, washed my dishes, washed my sheets so I'd have clean ones today. I slept atop the (aptly named) comforter that my stepmother (dad's second wife), Dyan, made for me when I was a teenager, to this day a most treasured gift. It is Fisher's favorite comforter, too, coveted by Chihuahuas and young man-boy alike, for burrowing under while we watch movies.

Brandi called last night while driving to massage school in Boulder, and in talking with her I felt as though drawn into another realm, one in preparation for my Journey today. I spoke of Light

Mother, how she comes to be of support to me with words and with touch. I spoke of how I feel such resistance when it comes to extending that love and compassion toward my father, to be able to truly embrace him as the little boy who is just doing the best that he can. Speaking of this with Brandi brought me to tears…then our connection got cut off, with her driving through the mountains and all. As I realized I was talking to quiet air, I stopped myself in the intense feelings coming up—I paused in them, took my ear buds out, crouched to the tile kitchen floor, and sobbed.

The painful stuff, I am not looking forward to, I do not wish to go back to again.

It is only a sensation, I am reminded by the voice which spoke the day after my first Journey, during my major freak-out break-down in the bathtub.

Remember, it is only pain, Light Momma says to me. It cannot kill me. It will pass. And the only way through it is through it, as they say.

Boy, I am really missing coffee right now.

* * * * * *

Second Medicine Journey
May 14, 2021
MDMA and Psilocybin
Intentions: Removing obstacles (third eye), opening to Spirit and Ancestors, to Animals, to the Divine and other-worldly. Connections with Nana, with Mother, with Father. To uncover what needs mending in order to help the "little girl" feel safe. Allow it to be so. Practice patience and forgiveness. Trust.

This Journey was performed at my house. I took the medicine as I lay in my bed with dogs and cat nearby.

Journey Notes (based on notes taken by Joan during the session, and others I contributed later):

9:00 a.m. – Took MDMA

9:30 a.m. – Listening to Transcendental Sound Meditation

9:50 a.m. – Me: "This is the point where I said last time that I can't believe I ever did this recreationally." Moving hands in gentle motions, placing them over my eyes.

Joan: "What are your hands saying?"

"I miss my horse…" Tears, tapping forehead with my fingertips. A small airplane flies over the house. "The airplane was my dad. I felt him here," I say.

10:00 a.m. – "I'm noticing that I'm not angry…there was a lot of resistance before…this feels a lot better. I was worried about you getting bored—weird," I say. Then the sing-song begins. "It's okay, Momma, you're safe. You're okay, Momma…" Seeing images of young Laura hiding in the tall wicker basket in the basement of the Bagley Parkway house, beneath the stairs, by the laundry chute. "It's okay, baby…What did she need?" I say to myself. "What do you need, baby girl?"

My eyes open, and attention shifts back to the present, to Joan, to the room. "The room seems smaller," I say to her. "Thank you for being here."

10:15 a.m. – Given dose of 1.5 g psilocybin.

I begin to feel the strong presence of my dad, my Nana, my mom. "I'm so glad you're here," I say to them, and let out a big sigh. Expressing love for my dad, telling him he did his best. "He was so sad," I tell Joan. Then, Lilah Jane—I feel the presence of my niece who passed when she was five weeks old. "Your momma misses you," I say to her. "Go to her and let her know you're safe."

Then, "Baby girl...Where are you?" I feel the presence of the child I miscarried. "You were just barely here," I say to her. "They gave me a rose for you at the Hoffman Process, and I cried..." (Just writing about this now finds me sobbing over my computer keyboard.)

"Dyan is here," I continue, "she had a hard life, too. Daddy, Momma, Nana, baby girl..." I felt surrounded by the presence of all who had come to witness and support me. "Light Momma. She's here when I need her, I just have to remember that. How can I feel safe?"

Joan: "See if she can show you."

"Honey, it's alright. It's hard, I know...I just want her to hold me," I say.

11:15 a.m. – I express that I want my animals to feel safe, before I can feel safe. "Mama wants me to feel safe," I say. "Daddy was so sad, he was so scared when she went away. Mama, can you help him? Can you help me? I want to feel safe, so I can help Fisher feel safe, too. Thank you, Momma. Thank you." I turn to Joan. "She says I'm doing a good job, and she's proud of me."

"I miss you, Momma. Daddy, I love you. It was so hard, and you were trying to do good...you did the best that you could. It's okay, Daddy, I'm okay. I am doing the best I can, too."

The presence of my mother tells me/shows me how my older sister felt she needed to protect all of us, so it has been hard on her..."Thank you, Mama, for showing me this," I say, "she's been trying so hard."

"I'm good, thank you, Mama...I'm good," I am saying (apparently she was asking how I am). "I just miss you. I miss you, too, Daddy. You had such a good heart."

"What do we need, Mama?" I let out a huge sigh. "Why weren't we enough for Daddy? Because he was scared. All that stuff the day he died…I didn't know what to do. I was scared, and angry. I said goodbye to his body as they wheeled it out the door—he wasn't in it anymore. Where is he? He's still here. Goodbye to his body—he was ready to let that go."

"He wants me to know that he loves me, and to feel safe. He didn't know how to feel safe…he meant well…Please help Ginny," I say, "and Wendy—she's doing well, but she misses you…"

"Oh, boy. This is a lot." I sigh, my hands moving gently above my chest, like waves.

Noon – "I feel tired. Is this what it feels like to feel safe?"

The notes say, "sleepy," and that I started getting nauseas/tired. I remember things taking a darker turn at this point. I was exhausted. "My mom says there is more about Mom stuff," I said. It feels a lot like being in labor again, in the hospital bed, with the baby not coming out. "I had a hard pregnancy. And I was nauseas a lot," I tell Joan.

Joan says, "Maybe ask inside if there is more your mom would like to show you."

I asked Anzu if she would help me. I felt Govinda's presence, too, and then that of my first (soulmate) dog, Camille. I had an awful headache, and felt terribly nauseas—it reminded me of being pregnant, of being so afraid that Fisher's dad would not be up for all of this, that he would leave me, and I'd be alone.

I spoke of an old roommate, Eirch, whom Wendy and I lived with in a cute little house on East Johnson Street in Madison, back in the early 1990s. The time that I was sick with stomach flu and basically passed out in the hallway right outside our bathroom door so I could be close to the toilet and throw up when I needed to. I remember opening my eyes to see Eirch with his head laid down on the floor in front of my face, tapping the tips of my upturned fingers gently, saying, "Laura, we're going to take you to the hospital now." I remember curling up in the back seat of his Volvo station wagon while he and his girlfriend (visiting from Portland) drove me through a snowstorm from one hospital to the next, trying to figure out where the ER was. I remember watching them bound through the snow and yellow streetlights of night, into the hospital's sliding glass doors, while I emerged slowly, head-first, from the Volvo's back door (wrapped in Dyan's comforter, as I was during the Journey, in my bed). I retched into a giant snowdrift, then retreated back to the warm confines of the purring station wagon's back seat, like withdrawing into a warm, safe womb. Later, in a quiet hospital room, hooked up to IV fluids, I remember Eirch and his girlfriend from Portland bringing children's books to read to me. This memory of Eirch taking care of me came with profound fondness and warmth, as I lay sick in my Journey bed.

Then another memory came to me, of the time Eirch heard a woman's voice talking to my cockatiels in my upstairs bed-room. "Pretty birds...nice birds...what pretty birds you are..." he heard her say. He thought the woman must be me, but when he climbed the steep, narrow stairway up to my room, nobody was there. When I got home from school later that day, he told me the story, and tears welled in my eyes. "You think it was your mom, don't you?" Eirch said to me.

"I know it was her," I replied.

Sometime later, I would tell this story to my dad, at which he began to cry. He told me that when he and my mom were first married, they lived in an apartment on the south side of Madison, and they had Zebra finches as pets. She used to stand by the cage and talk to them. "Pretty birds, nice birds, what pretty birds you are..." she would say.

In my Journey bed of memories and sadness, I struggled with feelings of overwhelm, of not wanting to be alone. I remember being concerned that Joan was not fully with me anymore, that she was distracted by other things—I asked her to please keep writing, I wanted her to take good notes, lest I forget all the images and insights that were being shown to me. I was cradling

Ashaya; she had become the baby that I needed to tend, but I was too sick (just like my mother with her daughters, I now realize)…I heard/felt my mother say to me, *Let her take care of the baby…* "Will you please take the baby?" I remember saying to Joan, climbing out of bed as she gathered Ashaya into her arms, cooing to her happily. I lurched to the bathroom, retched into the toilet, feeling my mother's presence surrounding me, enfolding and comforting me. Joan took care of Ashaya, the baby, as my mother took care of me.

I remember scooting on my butt down my carpeted stairs like a little girl, one step at a time, to the landing by the bookshelves, sobbing. At about 4:00 p.m., Joan brought the candle for me to blow out, closing ceremony, and I wailed because I was still full-on in it (though exhausted), and beside myself with grief. I thought she was getting anxious to leave. "It's okay," Joan said, "I'm not going anywhere. I will be here for as long as you need me." I cried some more, begging for a cup of coffee, "Please, please—can I have just a little sip?" but she would not oblige. I blew out the ceremony candle, then lurched for the master bathroom—my Dad's bathroom—where I purged and purged into the toilet, 'til there was nothing left to do but sob and heave, thinking/feeling, *FUCK THIS CANCER*—knowing it was my Dad, in me.

* * * * * *

Saturday, May 15, 2021
Sometime close to 9:30 a.m.

Bubbly water mixed with deep orange antioxidant juice blend bubbling in the glass set on the old, small desk in the guest room, where I write. The bubbling sound is so loud in the silence that it causes Ashaya to bark. Both dogs are a little on edge this morning, after the intensity of all our lying around yesterday. All the beauty and insight, the connection with the Spirit world, all the *thank you thank you thank yous* throughout the day. And then there were the awful parts, too. Where I wanted it to stop,

I wanted it to end—just thinking of it now brings a powerful hot flash and sweat to all my pores. *Oh, Momma, momma, momma,* I called—so sad, little baby girl—

Momma is with you, she is right here. Hush, now, baby girl–you are safe.

The hot flash subsides. A little bird chirps outside my open window. Titter and flutter and chirp.

"We did a good job," I said to Joan this morning on the phone. "I think we hit all the marks. I am curious to see how this will unfold over the next few weeks."

Right now, I just feel quiet and tired. I feel that today is a good day to just loll about gently, to rest and sleep some more, to reflect upon all the experiences and insights of yesterday. To feel grateful for my mother's presence now, I feel her close to me. So many visitors yesterday, those doors opened wide to step through. So much kindness, and compassion, and insight given and received... from asking Joan to take the baby so I could be sick and take care of myself, with Momma surrounding me (it's okay—the baby was safe). To retching in Dad's bathroom like a demon being expelled from me, and feeling my dad as he must have felt retching into that same toilet, feeling the fear and the anger, thinking, *fuck this cancer–get it out of me.* And Momma supported me, she held me as she must have held him. *Yes, now, allow this release.*

Anzu lays perched on the bed behind me, front paws crossed, gazing out the open window by my desk. When I turn to her, her gaze turns gently to me. We watch out for one another, that is what we do.

I need to sleep some more.

Momma says, *Yes, baby girl, why don't you go back to sleep. You are safe, I am here, sweet girl. Rest, now. You are safe.*

Sunday, May 16, 2021

Sometime around 5 a.m., sunlight is beginning to seep into the sky.

I awoke to the sound of air brakes from a semi-truck on the slope of the highway probably a mile away. I can only imagine what that sounds like in the fancy townhomes closer to that slope. Humans can be so curiously inconsiderate of others, it's truly a remarkable thing. Before five in the morning, and even with my windows closed (specifically trying to dampen the human sounds and lights, so I can sleep), this is what comes to me. Oh, my darlings—oh, Humanity—*what is it that you NEED?*

This feels like such an important and resonating question right now, for myself, and so importantly, for everyone around me—*WHAT IS IT THAT YOU TRULY NEED?* It feels like the most important question to ask, and to bear in mind continuously. To listen carefully to the intuitive sense in my heart, my body, my mind.

Ashaya has been a bit nervous and needy, and Anzu has kept a watchful eye on me. I thanked them for being present for me on Friday, for the long, intense day of them mostly laying around me, being my support team, dutifully, alongside Joan. Even Apollo came to lay on the end of the bed when I called to him, though he spent the first part of the day curled atop the propped-up single mattress beside Fisher's bed, the one that Fish likes to press himself against when he sleeps. The window was open, letting the fresh air in, and Joan reported that Apollo was curled comfortably there.

What is it that you need?

Ask, and listen quietly, gently.

What is it that I need?

I remember having beautiful, erotic dreams about Beorn. All of that is such a mystery to me. After writing to him yesterday morning about my Journey, and his brief but enthusiastic reply, my wheels have started spinning—yes, this is what I want, please, give me more of THIS. Connection. Passion. Desire.

Crazy hot flash rises. *Go get a banana and some water,* I hear.

Okay, tea and banana. Dogs have been out to pee, and cat sniffed around the back yard while I stood barefoot on my flagstone path and smiled up at the swallows tittering above me. The sky is all Easter egg blues and pinks, now turning yellow where the sun begins to rise. I open the windows so I can hear the birds tittering away outside, as cool morning air pours in. Apollo is being peskery now, yowling at me. I think maybe he needs to be outside.

Oh, sweet baby girl—what is it that YOU need?

I need to feel safe. Not alone.

* * * * * *

Another interjection from Modern Day Times:

At some point while I've been working on this project—this book—I thought of writing a chapter entitled "How to Not Write a Book." I don't know that the subject is truly worthy of an entire chapter (feeling defeatist to give it that much energy), but it does bear mentioning that somewhere high on the list of ways to Not Write a Book is to get a puppy. Which, of course, three weeks ago, I did. I have raised other puppies—Camille, Joey, Govinda, Anzu…and Ashaya, who was several months old when she came to us from that weird hoarding situation, but she was never house-trained, and very puppy-like in her needs—so I knew what I was getting myself into, that it would have some bearing on my availability to write. Last springtime I stopped myself from getting a horse, also knowing that the time and energetic (not to mention financial) commitment would leave me stretched too thin. I told myself and my editor that I will reward myself with a pony when the book is done and done. In the meantime, the canine-oriented maternal urges I've been keeping at bay since Govinda passed three years ago have finally caught up with me, in ways I tell myself are signs from the heavens. I won't go into the myriad examples of how perfectly the stars have aligned to bring just the right young soul-pup into my world…but I will tell you that I've named him Pony.

Even perfect puppies come with challenges, like human babies with their many needs. I could go on and on about these things; I could turn the course of this story into some bumbling of puppy-rearing lessons learned, and still learning. As Pony whines just a little in his crate not feet from me (Anzu, the puppy and I just in from our evening walk in the blowing snows, so he should settle pretty quickly), I remind myself of what I have learned and am still learning; back to that thing about Intuition, and trusting the guidance that Be. If the stars (or whoever) guided me to adopt this puppy, so shall they guide me to finish my story, in due time. When I think about quitting it, just setting this project down, I hear in my heart, my brain, and reverberating in my bones a resounding NO—*Nope, nada, nope, nope, noh—you are so close, Laura.* And Pony is a part of the story now. Pony is a part of the knowing.

I'm not even sure what that means, exactly, but it's making me smile, so I'll take it. I will keep taking this all as it comes, making it up as I go along.

This story, these journals. It's been more than a few weeks since I transcribed those last words about feeling safe and not alone, and I reckon I needed a little break. Some time and space to process these images and feelings, as well as time and space to focus on my day-to-day life; my business, my animals (including the kitten, Freyja, whom I adopted in the springtime, and the momma cat, Little Bear, whom I adopted some months after that), my Self, and my gloriously complex teenagery man-child.

So much of my life these days feels like living in some curious dream…a dream where I am a spirit in flesh clothing, getting to experience all the three-dimensional things. Where I get to time-travel by way of memories, by way of sorting through and visioning possible futures while my body sleeps. It's like swimming in a time-travel ocean, feeling the sway of waves and water and surface and sky, the shifts of reality. It is the being right here, right now, in my present experience which I find most challenging, and worthy of practice—surfacing into the present moment—when there are so many other interesting places (throughout time, and imagining, and remembering) to be.

Right here, right now, dogs all sleeping. Right here, right now, I type by dim light, the sun having set. The wise old cat, Apollo, grooms himself beneath the wooden table and plush fern. Little Bear asleep on my momma's old rocking chair, I suspect Freyja is upstairs in Fisher's room, watching the aquariums (nope—she is asleep on the dog bed beneath the table, at my feet). The wind blows cold outside the townhouse windows, and me…I feel grateful, I am grateful. Even the difficult time-travel ocean is worthy of diving back in, of gaining new depth of insights with each revisiting. Of allowing for guidance, for healing of every painful bit. This is how we grow our hearts stronger, every moment that we allow our hearts to grow…to open to the possibilities of love, of forgiveness, of strength, and courage, and grace. To open our lives to the letting another's love in, with all the blessed vulnerability love brings. Even when that other is a puppy born of challenged history, now safe in our comfortable home. Especially now, with the lessons this young Pony brings, it is time to let love in.

Right here, right now—it's time to trust what guides me onward in this plight, this journey, this telling of a story. While the puppy wrestles noisily with a deer antler in his crate, it is time to dive in again.

* * * * * *

Tuesday, May 25, 2021
5:27 a.m.

This morning in my email I found my Journey notes from Joan. I read them and thought—wow, that's all? For the entire day, and all that came pouring out of me—this is all she wrote? I know she is coming from a sincere place of helping, and also...I find myself wondering if this is going to work for me. Am I expecting too much? It's just that I feel there is so much more in those depths for me to get to, and I need serious assistance from outside of the well. I don't want to hurt Joan's feelings, and also...

I will ask for guidance around this.

Sit with this, no need to worry. The guides around me will help. Don't worry, Laura, everything is as it should be.

Yesterday, dropping Fisher at school, he told me he needed me to go back home to get his bicycle. I was spinning out, all whack-a-doodle. I texted Beorn, asking if he could talk in person. He replied, "Of course," but that he was at work, so could he call me in a bit. He asked if I was okay.

"Short answer—Yes." I replied.

When he called, I felt so relieved.

He was under a truck, removing winter parts to put summer parts on. He asked what I was doing, I told him I was delivering a bicycle that I wasn't even sure Fish needed, and going back home now to get my other rig for dog clients. We agreed it was nice to have two vehicles for different purposes, but that it's important to keep work gloves in each. It was good just to hear his voice, his laughter, to hear the comical little voices in which he sometimes says things, like, "Oh! Goats!"

When shifting to the meat of things, I told him that in the trauma work I'm doing, he is a huge trigger for me. He protested that he doesn't WANT to trigger me—and I told him it's good, actually, that this is what I need to address within myself. This is the stuff that's so important for me to work with now, so I can end the eternal wrestling with it all and move forward. So I can live the rest of my life in the ways I WANT to live, rather than encumbered by all of this unsorted baggage from my childhood. But I know it's a lot to put on him, I said, and I'm sorry, and I can disengage from him if it's too much. He said he gets it. He confided in me, struggles from his own early life—

"It affects our parenting," he said matter-of-factly over the phone, from beneath a truck.

Yes, of course it does. And the work doesn't stop with addressing it. The work continues for the rest of our lives.

I felt grateful to him for sharing with me that which I know is difficult to speak. It's a lot to open up about on a Monday morning, while lying on your back under a truck. He just wants frosting, he laughed, because it's delicious. We both laughed and agreed, for whatever that will look like—yep, frosting on the Special Friends cake.

Anyhoo...talking with Beorn helped me quite a bit, just that dose of connection, and laughter, and sharing of some uncomfortable feelings. Then he had to get back to focusing on work, which was fine, because really, I did, too.

I went trail running with dog clients, I ate a healthy lunch, I listened to a sound meditation for nearly an hour, then took a short nap. I connected with horses, cleaning stalls while listening to an inspiring podcast conversation between Rich Roll and Light Watkins; I forwarded it to Beorn, and thanked him for creating time for me. I told him he is a gem of a man, for all of his complexities. I told him I am grateful to count him as a friend.

Chapter 13
Butterflies

"Sure as I'm breathing,
Sure as I'm sad
I'll keep this wisdom in my flesh"

— Eddie Vedder, "No Ceiling"

Friday, June 4, 2021
11:00 a.m.

Sitting out on the back patio at the ornate metal "friendly place" table, as my Nana used to call the place out back by the swimming pool and canal, beneath a giant palm tree. Here, now, at my table (could this be Nana's actual table, which I inherited from Dad?), sun shining, birds singing, noisy little airplane buzzing around up in the sky. Anzu has lain down near me. She was excited when I first got out here, thinking I'd throw her the ball—but, noh—"Go lie down, please," I said to her. She is disappointed, but dealing with it well.

It's interesting how my complexion has really broken out from my glutenous, non-vegan, crappy eating this past week or more. It is not surprising, and a good reminder of the ways in which it's important to take good care of myself. My face and legs look swollen to me, and of course I feel all thick in the middle. Achy, bloated. This is me in a state of energetic imbalance, a state of emotional distress.

I want to write about my session with Joan this morning, about the IFS (Internal Family Systems) therapy method we used. I first learned of IFS through a Tim Ferris podcast interview with Richard Schwarz, the founder of the technique. The interview was earth-shaking for me at the time, the first public addressing of Tim Ferris' experience of being molested repeatedly as a young boy; he walked bravely through the revisitation of this trauma, with Dr. Schwarz's calm guidance. I was brought to tears in my kitchen, pausing to listen as they went through the process, completed with a visualization of Tim's little boy "part" of himself being carried to a place of his choosing—in this case, the adult Tim's home in the country. There, the little boy Tim can be safe.

The IFS with Joan was tough work for me, and VERY uncomfortable at times, but now I do feel a sense of relief, having come through the other side of this morning's session. Joan asked how I've been these past couple of weeks, and I told her it's been really rough; I've felt really ANGRY, broody, tired. I've been super compulsive and clingy toward Beorn, reaching out to him again and again, even when I understand that he needs some space; some room to process, and to deal with all the stuff on his own plate. Despite knowing this, I still get angry and frustrated with him for not being more available to me...then I get angry and frustrated with myself for being needy.

Guided by Joan, laying on the sofa beneath the weighted blanket, eyes closed...I feel a sensation in my abdomen, in my stomach. I feel deep sadness and pain. "What does it look like?" Joan asks, and I see—it is like a hole, a pit that goes down infinitely inside of me. It is black and swirling grey (is this the void I try to fill with food? With animals? With a man?). "Go to the little girl who feels this sadness, this pain," she tells me—and I am with her, the little girl Me who is somewhere between five and seven years old. It takes a little doing, but the little girl allows me to connect with her. I call upon my mother and Light Momma to come help her feel safe. My little girl is crying—so much sadness, so much fear. We surround her—I wrap my arms and spoon my body around her—like the safety of a womb on her little bed, in my childhood room at the house on Bagley Parkway Street. The little girl Me feels comforted, stops crying, just wants to sleep in that peace and safety…she just wants to go to sleep. Joan is still asking questions, asks the sleepy part if it can step aside—then I am crying again, sobbing, turning away from Joan with my arms raised in a protective posture around my head, covering my eyes.

I just want this to stop. I want this to go away, this pain.

Joan asks if the little girl can let her in, and the girl says to me, *No*—she doesn't trust her. The little girl wants to trust me, but isn't sure, doesn't understand how all of this works. *It's okay,* I say to her inside my head. I show her—I hold her—I am right here with her. Momma and Light Momma are here, too.

Joan asks if there's anything she wants to tell me, little girl, and she says it's Daddy—he is so angry, he is so sad. "Some of the time," Joan says, but the little girl corrects her—

"*MOST* of the time."

Little girl wishes she could fix Daddy, make him better, so he could love her. I laugh and tell her, *Yes, my darling—and you will still be trying to do that for the men in your life for a long time.*

Joan asks, "So what do you want to show this little girl now? What do you want to tell her?"

I hold the little girl in front of me, I hug her, and kiss her sweet face. *You are so strong and magical,* I tell her in my mind. *You are connected with the Animals, and the Earth. You feel your momma still around you, little girl. And now you can feel Me, and Light Momma, too. Oh, sweet child, you are so beautiful, and strong.* I take her by the hands, lift them up toward the sky; I hold her long arms lovingly as she smiles and stretches her fingers upward.

Oh, my darling girl, I'm so sorry your daddy can't be there for you. I'm so sorry he's too angry and afraid. He is so sad that it makes him not able to see you, but that is NOT YOUR FAULT. It is not fair for a little girl to feel frightened and alone, and I am sorry, so sorry, my sweet child. Oh, sweet baby girl, I am here now, you are safe. Look, see? Anzu is here...and Camille...and your Mindy, too. It's okay, baby girl—we are all here, and we all love you.

We all will keep you safe.

Joan asks if there is someplace the little girl wants to go where she can feel safe. I laugh, "Yes, she wants to go to Tim Ferris' farm, to hang out with his little boy there." So that is where we go—or at least how we imagine it; with green fields and trees, beautiful red barns, ponds, and streams. With animals all safe and happy and well-tended. What a truly lovely place.

Joan asks if there is anything the little girl Me wants to bring—she wants to bring Mindy (we start crying again), so Mindy will be safe from Daddy and his sadness, and his rage. So, we gather up Mindy, and some favorite stuffed animals, and a couple pretty dresses...we go to Tim Ferris' farm, where my little girl is delighted to befriend his little boy, to take him by the hand, to visit all the animals, to play in the grass and trees...in this magical place where everyone is safe, and happy, and loved.

I find myself smiling as I write this. Anzu is stretched out in the sunny grass of our tiny townhouse yard. She sighs, and closes her eyes.

Back on the couch, Joan asks if there is anything else the little girl wants to leave behind from the other place—

Yes, she says. The anger, the sadness, the fear.

"And how would she like to get rid of it?" Joan asks, "What element would she like to release it to? To the earth? To the wind? To water? To fire?"

I wasn't sure what I was seeing, then – a darkness, like a wind sucking…like layers in a dark, black-and-grey speckled stone… then I realized, it was the black hole, the void, the abyss in the core of me. Release it all to that, I thought. Let it be sucked far away, forevermore. Let that abyss be filled, be closed, be gone. Let this pain torment me nevermore.

Tiny Ashaya lays on the flagstone pathway now. A bird sits on the feeder, cracking seeds, chirping to us or whomever. Anzu rises, gets her tennis ball, sits back down. There is a perfect light breeze of summertime rolling down from the distant mountains. I still have a soft smile on my face. This afternoon I have barns and paddocks to clean, I have several creatures to tend. Right now, I feel like going for a little bike ride to stretch my legs, to move my long limbs. In any of the number of ways I can show nurturing and kindness to that little girl in me, let it be so…that she may grow up strong, and kind, and wise in this troubled world. That she may understand the fear and pain of others in this lifetime, that she may know how to ease their suffering; how to embrace them, how to guide them in their own healing. How to help others recognize and express their own beauty, their value, their strength. Let ALL beings feel this safety, this peace, this balance, this bliss.

In the grass, Anzu sighs once again. In my lap now, Ashaya does the same.

Tuesday, June 8, 2021
Sometime after 6:30 a.m., because that's when I got up, thankful to have slept again past five.

Yesterday was very long and full, and I was very, very tired. Reaching out to Beorn again after his little burst of enthusiasm when I texted that I'd found myself milking a lovely goat (restrained in a stanchion, contently munching grain) and wondering if he owns handcuffs. He does, he replied excitedly. He then gushed about how, after the end of his last relationship, he decided he'd like to explore more "freedom" with his sexual expression. Ah, joy! And lucky for me, I figured. I wanted to continue that conversation with him, but as happens so often, suddenly he was gone, disappeared from my small screen of enticing text messages. Enough interaction from him for one night, apparently; I have been divvied up as much attention as he had at the moment to give. Leaving me to wonder, as I do.

What beliefs drive me?

What is it that I need?

I feel as though I am not taking it quite so personally as I once did. Even if it's that he's not particularly into me, that's fine, and more about him than me—it's just how things go, sometimes. It is the imbalance part which I find difficult; the wanting to connect with him when his part is of needing space to do his thing. I believe that with most of my relationships, this has arisen as a theme. There are partners who stand out in my mind as desiring a great deal of connection, and while I deeply appreciated those offerings (didn't I? From their perspectives, those men may beg to differ), I ended each of those relationships, eventually. With Ryan, our finale was in a flurry of frustrated rage—one which I did not intend to end things, ultimately, but that was the way things went. Curiously, when one hollers at their partner to *get the fuck out* (despite a closetful of abandonment issues, or, more honestly, because of them), and the partner leaves, sometimes they never return… At least not to the one who was hollering at them, which is totally understandable. What we could call the setting of clear boundaries.

From our son, it must be noted in no uncertain terms—he has truly never left.

Perhaps this is my self-fulfilling prophecy, to push men until they leave me; to challenge them to do so, until they finally do. Huh. I don't know. I do know that right now my heart of hearts keeps reminding me that reaching out to Beorn as often as I do is not in my own best interest. He's shown me repeatedly that what he is up for is connection in little fits and starts, while requiring a world of space. Why does that raise so much anxiety in me? Daddy stuff, for sure. Needy little girl stuff. Afraid that he will not see me, honor me, appreciate me for who I am. Afraid that he will leave me for another girl in whom he finds more value.

I remember at Dad's funeral, one of his friends from Rotary spoke of how she always felt so *seen* by him. I felt envious, struck by how he could offer that gift to another young woman, yet it was rarely felt by me.

A close friend from high school attended the funeral, and he said to me later with great sincerity, "Who was that woman even talking about in there? I remember your dad being *terrifying*."

Maybe there was just too much from my childhood to make up for, for me to allow any sense of being seen by my dad. Maybe it was me never really forgiving him, never fully trusting him, or letting him in. Maybe that is why I am still mired in this anxiety, this apprehension around any man who truly catches my attention, who holds my affections. This is the mystery I am still trying to unravel, to resolve after all these years.

What does my little girl need?
To feel safe (protected).
To feel loved.
This is a lot to ask of any man, particularly at the beginning of a Relationship…

…or really, ultimately, *IS IT?*

Thursday, June 10, 2021
6:30 or so, a.m.

Slept pretty awfully last night, was awake for nearly two hours while the trucks did their noisy 1 a.m. and 2 a.m. visitations to the transport warehouse across the field, then lumbered all grumbly away. I had my windows wide open even though I knew the trucks would wake me up, I still needed them wide open, I still needed the night air and sounds of crickets pouring in.

Wow, this morning I find myself in tears again...I honestly am not sure where this is coming from, but I would really like to discover whatever it is that's troubling me so deeply. I would really like to heal whatever wound this is, which obviously still needs to be healed.

Oh, my Spirit Guides and Helpers. Oh, Badger spirit, oh, Bear spirit, oh, Horse spirit. Oh, Momma, Nana, Light Momma—pretty please and thank you. Thank you for your presence in this curiosity of three-dimensionality. Thank you for gently guiding me through.

I am reminded of the vision I had on the sofa, laying with eyes covered, listening to the sound meditation, waiting for Beorn to arrive on Mother's Day, and not entirely sure that he would. When he got here, my mind was still swimming with it, with the images and sensations of being born, of being carried from my mother's body. I told him I'd been having a dream, but that was only how I could explain it to him. It was more than just a dream. And this was nearly a week before my second Journey, so the medicine from my first Journey would have been well out of my system by then, the vision was in no way chemically induced. "That's intense," Beorn had said, and I agreed. This experience, this memory, this re-creation (or whatever one would call it) of being born, on Mother's Day.

Right now, I realize that another Radiohead song has been playing in my mind since I woke up for the final time this morning. The time when I decided to stretch my toes to the ceiling and wiggle my feet around, to run my hands up my long legs, noting the small scratches and bruises from yesterday, from a good day's work in the sun.

Ice age come and ice age come, this is really happening...

Okay, yes, thank you, Spirits—I get it. You really like Radiohead, don't you?

I hear the immediate answer in my noggin, and it makes me smile:

YES.

This is the opening. This is the rebirth, as many times as you desire it, child. This is your experience in this lifetime, three dimensionality, however you should choose it. This is really happening, child, this is all the experience for you...What do you choose? This is your movie, baby girl. This is your Experience, your Life. This is exactly what you came here to do, this is what you came here to Be. This is what you came to engage with, along with all the others who are a part of this, a part of You—a part of this grand, mass Experience, if you will. Yes, this is really happening, because that is what you CHOOSE.

My body (my stomach), my three-dimensional vessel tells me it's time to make some beans.

Ice Age come and Ice Age come.

Ashaya trembles in my lap. I fold my strong fingers around her, I caress her tiny body, ears, and limbs. She settles back in, no longer trembling. Like me, all she needs is to feel supported, loved. All she needs is to feel safe.

This is really happening.

* * * * * *

When Brandi and I spoke on the phone the other day, she mentioned that she's been wanting to make time to journal— that she understands the potential benefits of it, but when she sits down to write, she has a hard time with it. I told her, oh, my gosh, for me it's like I can't NOT write. That if I could spend a solid two hours writing every morning before sunrise, with a hot cup of goat milk coffee on the desk, close at hand—ah, what a happy camper I would be. How many mornings have slipped away without me realizing, as the words pour from my pen? How many mystical realms have I been led to? How many insights have I gained? If I don't get to write, I feel agitated, as though I am missing something primary and part of me. Like a runner who misses their daily run. Like a giant aquatic angel beast trapped in a swimming pool, longing for the sea.

"It's like your therapy," Brandi observed astutely. "It's like you get your own little therapy session at the beginning of every day."

Yes, I agree whole-heartedly. It is precisely like that.

* * * * * *

June 19, 2021
(Facebook rant)

Times are always "interesting," as my dad would say—always Interesting. People, places, beloved animals come and go. It can feel difficult to know what to do with all of that sometimes, how to feel about it all…to feel it truly, deeply, but without any pain—Nope, that's not how it's going to roll. I miss my dad, I miss my horse, I miss my mom, and dear friends who have gone away. I believe that is all good and well, and as it should be; to touch that feeling as it rises, to hold it gently for a while. To cradle that sadness, that depth of emotion. Allow it to rise warm and full, like an ocean in my chest. To love it, to love them so deeply…then to release it, and move on. To release them, and move on.

Monday, June 21, 2021
4:50 a.m.

I hear a semi-truck out there across the field, it's backin' up, beeper all beepin' away. What an affront to the glorious delicacy of early morning. I slept curiously, all my dreams blending with reality, the surreal nature of knowing that we are setting out for Wisconsin today, also flooded with the images and reverberating sensations of the man who arrived once again in my driveway, giving me butterflies. Who came in my front door, wound his strong arms around me, seeming as though he would like to eat me whole. Ah, so delicious, to press against this other set of strong limbs, this other strong body. Ah—that which I have missed, which I have craved since our encounter on Mother's Day. Now on Father's Day, we become lovers, well suited to each other in that regard. To have him all around me, above me, beneath me, beside me...To see what looks like gentle sincerity in his eyes. To feel his strength, and his vulnerability. Opening my eyes to see him cradling my folded legs in a loving embrace, kissing the tops of my knees. So gentle, so beautiful, so kind, and caring. So much a mystery, unfolding in tiny bits at a time. So much of my own mystery, unfolding gently inside of me. To allow myself that vulnerability.

Before now would have been too soon for us, in our curious dance since last autumn.

Now, we will see.

I thanked him as we lay quietly, motionless, together like puzzle pieces made of clay.

"For what?" he asked.
"For being here. For being with me."

This morning there is all the final Getting Ready to do, then to pick up Fisher from his dad's. Tonight, we will stay in a hotel somewhere in Nebraska, I reckon. Tonight, I wonder if the taste of Beorn will still linger on my lips, or if it will just seem like a dream again. This dream of living beautifully, powerfully, sensually. This dream of being so very alive, and awake.

Thursday, July 15, 2021
6:18 a.m.

Three steps forward, two steps back.

"You look beautiful," she said across the marble of the bar looking in on my kitchen counter, where I peeled and chopped carrots and beets from Bear and his wife's farm. I felt as though I was too far away from her, especially with her sadness and awkwardness, and the dark circles under her eyes. I listened as I cut and peeled. I heard and felt every word. There were moments when I paused, my gaze turned to her, my attention entirely on her words. There were moments when tears rose to my eyes and goosebumps to my flesh. Throughout the conversation and the listening, there was a tightness in my chest.

Who hurt you, little girl?

The echoing question in my mind. Who hurt my beautiful friend? Who hurt me? How do we get to them? How do we cleanse them, tend to them? How do we allow them to mend? *How do we allow ourselves to mend?*

There was not enough time to dive into exploring these questions with her—she had arrived in a flurry from an appointment she'd been late for, still on her phone as she approached my back sliding-glass door, exchanging I Love Yous with whoever that was. When she had to leave my home, she was already late for her next call or meeting or whatever. All the flurry and fluster and rushing are difficult for me when they arise in my own life, so I tried to just focus on letting go of any attachment or judgement or resentment around her whirling from one commitment to the next, from one interaction to the next. A fluttering butterfly who touches down on me for just a moment—I guess that makes me a flower. I straighten up, I hold mostly still. I try to be present for our interaction, for our brief time of connection. I try to gage our remaining time together and share appropriately, to ask heartfelt questions, and to listen. Like a good flower, like a good friend. Until the wind of her next commitment stirs her dusted, weary wings...until that flurry comes, lifting her away from me again.

Right now, I realize that I have the Elliot Smith song "Independence Day" in my head again—the line about the butterfly (which to me had always been about my Midwestern muse)—and a rising feeling of wanting to cry.

Who hurt you, little girl?

Jesus—**what?**

What is this pain, and how do I release it so I can get on with my life?

Later in the morning, I had this horrible, fucked-up moment in the rain, pulling up in front of a new cat clients' house to meet for an initial interview. I saw a beautiful couple walking toward me down the sidewalk as I parked on the other side of the road. They were holding hands, smiling, the guy holding a leash attached to a pretty little pit bull's harness. The gal had long, bleached-blond hair with fashionably grown-out roots, wearing black eyeliner in the way of female pop stars of our time. She was very pretty, in a pop-culture sort of way. The fellow was tall beside her, and well built, one could see, even beneath his thick flannel and hoodie pulled over his head against the rain. I had a weird moment where I thought all of the sudden, *Oh, my God–is that Beorn?* The man's face was obscured to me beneath his hood, the shadows revealing only sharp lines of a beautiful nose, and scruff or a beard which maybe was too dark to be Beorn's. I sat in the truck with ice coursing through my veins, waiting for the couple to pass across the street. They were no longer holding hands, and the fellow must have felt my intent gaze from afar, through rain-streamed windows. He looked my direction, then quickly looked away. *What the fuck*, I thought. *Am I losing my fucking mind?* My thoughts raced through all the reasons why it could not be him, how it didn't line up...unless he was being deceptive, after all. Unless all his "busyness" and unavailability was because he was dating this other, fancier, younger gal, too (an experience I'd had with another man not too distantly in my past—the feeling still fresh enough to sting), and he was going to dump me for her. And I have been chumped, once again.

Oh, my darling, my precious little girl. Who put these stories in your head? That you are so replaceable, unlovable, unloved? That the man you adore and desire to be cherished by will always leave you for someone you see as more desirable than you? Where does this come from, and, more importantly, how can we let this go? Because this definitely does not serve you.

Thinking about it now brings a wave of nausea, makes me feel swoony and sick. I continued to feel as though I was losing my mind and could not shake the images, the story I'd created. Part of me knew that it could not have been Beorn, that if it were him, I would have known it. Still, the experience felt deeply troubling, surreal, and by the time I got through my interview with the clients and their cat and got home, I was nearly spinning out. There was a part of me nagging and persistent, refusing to release that fear. *What fuckery is this?* I hated it, the questioning. I just wanted it to go away. The only way I could resolve it, I finally decided, was to ask him directly. Just do it. Just tell him of my horrible moment, and ask if he is seeing anyone else.

His quick reply to my text message: "No. Why?? What horrible moment?"

Oh, my God, the relief I felt at his typed words. Also, the shame and fear at having bothered him with this, with my insecurities, in the midst of everything he already carries around.

Fuck.

Yep, that's another thing for me to look at, for sure—why I feel as though I am a burden to him. Why I would choose to put energy toward someone who I feel I am a burden to? Just what am I trying to resolve here? I'm sure I don't need to dig too deep to find the answer inside me.

Sweet Mother, this is all a lot.

I told him about the beautiful couple, about the dog, and how I couldn't shake the feeling that maybe it had been him, that I just had to be sure. "Sorry," I wrote. "Flashbacks to challenging times past. Not you."

He replied, "Well, I'm at my friend's house having a beer with him. So…nope."

I reached out a little further, suggesting he should come by. "Can't. Busy chaos and full throttle." He wrote.

Yes—this is what I have come to anticipate from him, not moseying down the sidewalk with a pretty little pit bull and girl. This intensity and full-throttleness. This hitting the ground hard and running, after pausing for a beer with his guy friend. This man who resides mostly in my imagining; elusive, strong, and brooding. This wild animal, this Wolverine.

This morning, always compelled to express myself, I reached out to him again. "Thank you for your patience with me, Beorn. This Self Work continues to bring up Interesting things…Feels like I'm in the Matrix sometimes, with Oracles baking cookies, and Buddha children bending spoons and all. Intense, sometimes uncomfortable. And all for the greater Good."

There you go, my darling. Now that experience has been processed, so the next practice is that of Releasing it, of Letting it Go. How about if you do a little two-week Beorn fast? Cut those chords, let that connection breathe, and rest. It is good practice for you, not to mention being a loving thing to do for him, to give him the space he needs. Your beloved child comes home to you this evening, giving you the perfect gage of two weeks. Focus on Fisher, on your own care and his. Focus on both of your needs. Yes, good—that sounds like the perfect idea, starting NOW—to lovingly let go of this beautiful, complicated Wolverine, and all that he carries. Right now, to lovingly RELEASE.

So good.
Now, Go.

Brandi says she will be my accountability partner on this.

Also, I saw another deer this morning, no doubt with a message for me. I look up "deer" in the Spirit Guides book. Deer represents Gentleness.

Gentleness and ease are exactly what I require right now, with myself, as well as with all who cross my path.

Perfect.

Chapter 14
No More Fucking Around

"This is how my heart behaves."

— Feist, *The Reminder*

Tuesday, July 20, 2021
6:24 a.m.

"The more you push, the more it pushes people away." I remember Ryan saying this to me many years ago, as I thrashed in the rabbit-snare of having lost our little family, and any hope of ever making things right. I pushed and pushed and pushed, as I do, as I have done. Trying desperately to fix it; trying to force clay into the shapes I desired and demanded, my hands losing their ability to hold the form, only to squash it in my desperation, to crush it into mangled lumps.

And here, I've done it again.

Why would I want to be with someone who does not appreciate me? Who does not naturally treat me in ways I feel I deserve to be treated? Why do I struggle to form these lumps of clay into some shape they don't naturally take? When there is so much resistance, so much struggle, so much WORK on my part.

After reading my words, Beorn texted back to me that we had better call it, better end it now "before there is any further hurt," he said, "that is the opposite of what I hoped for." This was not the answer I wanted to hear—what I wanted was for him to be available for at least a conversation on the subject. For him to say, "I understand that you are in a vulnerable state, and your friendship is important to me. Our connection is important to me. Your feelings are important to me." I would have been placated; I would have felt soothed. Instead, as I perceived it, he was just bowing out, denying me—he was abandoning me, taking his love away. Just like my mother, even if it wasn't her fault. Just like my dad, right up to his dying day.

Beorn has certainly come into my life at a tumultuous time, a time when, as Joan once put it, my snow globe is all shaken up. What a chaotic mess I can be, especially on the inside. My frantic desire is to reach out for something to cling to—for someone to cling to—as I'm tossed about in the waves of this, as I feel my head being pulled under. Let me breathe, oh, let me cease my thrashing! Let me remember how to let go, now, how to flow. Please, oh, please, let me remember. I do not want to be Chaos Girl. I do not want to push those I love away.

What came to me is this:

Okay, so here's the thing, Laura:
Beorn is not ready for this, he is not in a place for this.
He is struggling with his own inner drama, quite literally.
He is afraid, feels overwhelmed,
and is trying to find his meaning, purpose, and peace.
He is breaking under the weight of it,
and has such a hard time letting others in—
TRULY in.
This is his boulder to roll up the hill,
to watch it tumble down again.
This is his choice right now, with what he knows in this moment.
Just like your dad as he was preparing to die—
In his fear and doubt and inner torment
he was only able to do

what he was able to do.
It does not mean that your dad does not love you,
or that Beorn does not care for you.
Only that he is not currently in a space
to express that love
in a way that you desire.
Honor their paths, and their struggles.
Honor their frightened inner child.
They are doing the best they can with what they know
right now.
They are struggling to find their own peace.
It is not to be found in the admiration and affections of others for them,
any more than it is to be found in THEM for you.
Remember this. Feel it.
Let the grasping go, let the struggling go, sweet child.
Remember who you are.

Tumultuous: adjective.
    Making a loud, confused noise, uproarious.
    Excited, confused, or disorderly.

What I believe I've learned from these past several months (if not from my entire freakin' dating history) is that I need to either be DATING someone—with very clear communication around intentions with such an exploration—or decidedly NOT dating them. I require SUPER DUPER CLEAR BOUNDARIES.

"No more fucking around," as Rolando recounted having told me in a dream, several years ago.

NO MORE FUCKING AROUND.

Even with the understanding of "casual but monogamous," apparently, I still needed more connection, more and very **clear** communication around what we both really want and need.

"Space" is one thing, but I guess it was just way too much "space" for my comfort. So that is done. Moving on. Let Beorn go, really and for real, this time. Let him ride off into the sunset upon his noble steed ... because this is obviously not a scenario that really works for me.

Learn the lesson. Turn the page.

Now, back to addressing that crazy hole in my heart, unfillable by any man.

Wednesday, July 21, 2021
6:31 a.m.

Hummingbirds on the feeder in the rising sunlight. I am still marveling at the magic of yesterday, floating down the river, laughing, holding out my hand to literally have a big, green dragonfly land on my finger, to ride there with me down the stream. *"Do you see it?!?"* I'm sure I must have asked my new friend, Sixxis, more than once, wanting to be sure he bore witness to this miracle. Fisher was floating a little ways behind us, so I don't know if he could see it. I must look up "Dragonfly" to see what it represents.

It was one of those moments, one of those afternoons which felt otherworldly, like a dream. There were moments when I had to remind myself to just stay present, stay in it, don't worry about it ending, or going south. As we pulled ourselves from the river, took off our PFDs to stretch and press our bodies fully against the warmth of the boulders in the afternoon sun, Sixxis kept laughing and exclaiming things like, "What magical place is this?! Is this really real?!" Such a change of scene and energy from where he had come, in Oakland, California. We had our fill of floating down the stream (hand-in-hand at first, as I'd been afraid of the current) through the play holes which made me shriek, then back out laughing to run upstream and do it all again. Like joyful otters, only in our clunky PFDs. Fisher and his friend were warmed by their wet suits, so kept doing laps and rounds, kept jumping in the river with their friends, with hollers and shrieks of joy. I settled myself on a huge, warm boulder by the boat ramp, in my cutoff shorts and black, cotton sports bra, stretched out like a lizard in the sun. Sixxis sat on another boulder up to my left, using the wet life vest to cool his beautiful, dark skin, and to shield him from the sun. We lounged, speaking excitedly about things Real and Meaningful...and I thought to myself, *Why, yes–thank you, Universe–**this** is **exactly** what I need.*

What a blessing—what a remarkable gift. With impeccable timing, after spending a sad morning crying on the phone to my dear friend, Lee, in Arizona—which, in itself, I am so very grateful for. Getting off the phone feeling, validated, appreciated, and adored. Feeling the sense of safety that I so desperately crave—like going through the play hole in the river, the waves pulling me under, but then—my hand held securely by a strong and laughing man, by this stunningly lovely new friend.

Oh, my goodness, what a day.

What a Super Interesting life this is.

Friday, July 23, 2021
6:37 a.m.

I awoke from dreams, then lay in bed, crying...dreams of being pressured, forced into sex. An act which should represent the deepest connection, respect, and love. I suppose this is what's coming up for me now around the whole Beorn thing; the withholding of genuine connection, and truthful, flowing communication. Perhaps these things are too frightening, hence, too difficult for him. So, the sex becomes just that—SEX—a lustful, empty act. Not its potential, or what I believe it is designed to be—an opening of doors to another magical realm, of peace, and sharing. Of ecstasy, laughter, deep sighs, and connectedness. Of downright fucking Bliss (no pun intended, but really).

We humans with all our trauma, with all our closed-off, dopamine-seeking fits...Way to go and spoil this gift, humans.

This is not what I wish for.
This is not what I choose.

And yet, looking back on my experiences of romantic love and sexuality, this is what I have somehow drawn to me. Right back to my earliest days of falling in love, of sharing my heart and body with boys, or with my first young man...what an emotional clusterfuck that all was. My heart feels seized and gasping, just thinking of it now.

Oh, boy, I guess there's a lot of baggage to unpack, yet.

Meanwhile, today, in my modern-day current experience of being an "adult," this thing of being Light in an aging, desiring, body made of clay. What is all this, and what do I do with it? This moment now, and the next. Feeling these feelings, uncomfortable as they may be. Unpacking past baggage in hopes of clearing all that away—of airing it out, the must and dirt and grime. Hanging all that crap out in the sunshine, that I may illuminate my very soul, become naked and free of all these burdens. Let it be light, let it be free. Let me be who I truly am in there, unburdened by the cracking clay. Unburdened, radiating only light and love. Is that possible? Or does that happen only when we shuffle off this mortal coil? That this is the grand adventure of Life, to experience all the struggle and strife, that we may decide it's not quite what we're up for. That we may decide what we'd rather is Light.

It is no coincidence at all that I am drawn to the strong and broody (yet charming, and often hilarious) men, who show themselves ultimately to be emotionally unavailable. The ones who show me just a little of their inner depth, and allude to their guarded vulnerabilities. This is the recipe for intrigue for me—the wanting to endear myself to them, that they may deem me worthy of loving, and truly letting in. This is also my perfect recipe for disaster, as what results (nine times out of ten) is a jumbled mess of insecurities, from which no one can allow for free-flowing, reciprocal and balanced love, in the end.

Huh. I wonder what is to be done about that.

I think it may have something to do with the ol' Letting Go and Letting Flow thing. With the ol' Releasing of Expectations around all of that. With the ol' Feeling of the Uncomfortable Feelings, neither suppressing them nor pushing them away...The Welcoming of Mara to Tea, as the Buddhists say. The Letting it all Be.

The Patience.
The Forgiveness.
The Trust—
Yes. Practice these.
Nothing really to Do in all of this, but so much really to Be.
Be Light.
Be Love.
Be Forgiveness, Compassion, and Peace.

And there we have it, my darling, the wisdom to be gleaned from all of this. No more fucking around, now, you see? This is why you are in this body. This is why you have that great big **feeling** heart of yours. This is why there is all of this. To feel. To learn. To love. To be.

All of this.

Chapter 15
Paying Attention,
and
Journey Number Three

Friday, October15, 2021
6:00 a.m. or so

There's this idea that we are—that I am—supposed to do something ***important*** with our lives, with my life. That I am compelled to do so. That I am somehow falling short if I do not embark on a journey of some great magnitude, and furthermore, to succeed. That I will have lived an unfulfilled (unworthy?) life... when sometimes (often) just checking all the boxes on my simple lists of daily Things to Do seems overwhelming—when there seems too much TO DO, and not nearly enough time to just sit quietly, to just sigh deeply. Just to feel, just to BE.

What are the most important things in Life?
If the needs of basic survival are met, *then* what?

Right now, certainly, my needs of basic survival are met, so my greatest challenge becomes when I get lonely. My desire for true and deep connection, in a world where I feel awkward and out of place. For true and deep connection with another human being who is much like me…and also different in ways that would complement one another, I suppose. All the stuff and the things. The companionship, the comradery.

It is GOOD for me to have this quiet Alone Time to myself—that is for certain. To rise gently in the mornings, sip my coffee, and write. When Fisher is here, it feels so good to know he is up there sleeping. That when the sun rises, he will rise, too, as will the dogs. It is important that I get to sleep early, that I may rise early enough to have this time to myself. In my perfect world (which this is not—so many tantalizing distractions from all angles), if I can head to bed around seven, then read until eight, and lights out—that will work. Nine hours seems about what I need to sleep right now. When I do my next Journey, I know it will be more for a while. Last night I read the book *Dopamine Nation* until twenty to nine, woke up on my own at twenty to six.

So. There we have it.

This loneliness—it is an interesting thing.

My session with Joan yesterday was good, a good stepping back in. We did not go super deep, did not do any IFS, I did not lay down and conjure up any tragic and traumatic childhood memories. We talked, just talked. Mostly I talked, really, and she listened, as any good therapist would. She made appropriate, insightful comments from time to time, she asked appropriate questions. I mused at how it was like the podcast interviews I love to listen to; people talking about their experiences and what they know. This is what a good, grown-up conversation can look like. It was what I needed, to be certain; to lean back in, to re-establish the trust. I can feel the Protector in me observing our interactions closely…Watching. Listening. Considering.

It will be fine, I tell it.
Thank you for protecting me.
This will be fine. Joan is good.

She looked particularly beautiful to me yesterday.

This happens sometimes with Brandi, when we are having especially good and deep conversations at her home, or out to coffee. These moments when she looks so stunningly beautiful to me that it is almost distracting, as though some God-light is illuminating her from the heavens, or—more accurately—that it is shining from within. I can see it, I can feel it in those moments, the God-light. I can almost hear the freakin' angels sing.

Joan reminded me to be very attentive to the needs of the part in me who is the little girl; who feels so awfully alone and undervalued, as though there must be something wrong with her. The weird-o, the crybaby, the bothersome pain-in-the-ass. The one who did not get loved-on or hugged, nor shown that she had value and worth. She was told/taught to be independent, to take care of herself. She learned to fight with her sisters for what she wanted, what she needed. She learned to be afraid of repercussions from her father. She learned to hide, to wait in fear for what would come. She learned she had to do things on her own, because no one could be trusted to help her. She learned to be wary, that "Life's not fair!!" as Dad would growl at us through bared, clenched teeth. And it's certainly not safe, this life.

Oh, my, how he had his struggles, to be sure. I spoke a lot in our hour about Dad. When the love of his life died so young, leaving him with three little girls to care for—that was one bum deal, for sure. I understand now that he became suicidal at the time, not knowing what to do without my mother. And toward the end of his life, Joan reminded me, he became very childlike and fearful, himself. Maybe he did not feel loved and seen by his own parents as a child. Maybe he did not feel safe. I don't know much about his relationship with Nana and Big Daddy, but I understand full well that everyone brings their own baggage to the table. Perhaps I could talk with my uncle, whom I adore—my dad's youngest brother—see what he remembers of their childhood, and the family dynamics there. It seems obvious to me that Dad had some need to be the Savior, the Knight in Shining Armor to the women he loved, which took a great deal of his energy and focus. He needed to feel valued, validated by his mates, and by others.

But his daughters? It is possible that I just did not catch on, but it did not seem evident to me that we were held in the same regard, though he boasted to others about how strong and independent we girls were, about how proud of us he was.

For our independence.

Oh, the irony. The flip side of "independence" being that I, for one, had a hard time feeling truly present with my dad in the end, when *then* he so wanted connection—after his young wife divorced him, and he moved to Colorado to be close to we girls, among John Denver's Rocky Mountains. I know my dad just wanted to feel appreciated, validated, supported, and loved—just as we all desire, as we all really need.

This is all a lot to consider.

And I have a full day ahead of animals to tend, so I'd best get off my booty and get to the duties at hand.

It bears mentioning—

Last night in my dreams, I had a romantic connection with Lenny Kravitz…ah, yes. That was LOVELY. Just to be near him, to feel the spark of mutual admiration and curiosity, with the added bonus of becoming friendly with Lisa Bonet, as well, as of course in my dream they were still close. Yes, yes, indeed. These dreams, they fulfill some underlying need from waking life.

Wednesday, October 20, 2021
5:36 a.m.

It is ridiculous—utter silliness—that I stubbed my toe so hard last night while walking from the kitchen during our co-parenting family Zoom meeting. I had left the little stool by the cupboard when putting away beans earlier, the one that Grandpa Kiner made. Dang, that hurt, and I wanted to holler, but I did not wish to interrupt the meeting, so instead I wrenched myself up in silent agony and allowed the pain to pass (as so many humans do). By bedtime, however, it had gotten much worse, and worsened yet through the night. Had not great sleep at all–pretty stinkin' lousy, tell truth—between the throbbing toe, hot flashes, and images of Great Pyrenees dogs coming at me...

Wowza, what a night.

I remember sobbing in bed at one point, triggered by some sad image in my dreams, though I'm not sure now what the image was. Soooo many images in my foggy mind, floating, drifting in and out with dreams and half sleep. At one point I was spooned around Anzu, feeling her chest rise and fall, hearing her breath. Feeling so deeply in love with her, the way I was with Camille...I remember marveling when I was younger, how it seemed that with each year passing, I loved Camille more and more. Was it a disservice to her that my attention, my affections were to become dispersed among two other dogs? Between Joey and Zeek, I mean. She was fond of Joey the Rat Terrier, whom I got as a puppy when Camille was six years old—they played well and enjoyed each other, as I recall. I do not remember so much how she felt about Zeek, whom I adopted impulsively from an over-crowded shelter in Northern Wisconsin; a gorgeous, sweet, Husky/Hound mix, with an ill-fitting cast on his broken leg. When I laid eyes on him, it was love at first sight -- I used to joke that he was my "danger boyfriend" dog. Camille was probably 14 years old by the time Zeek came into our lives...in full honesty, he was to be her replacement. He was to ease the unbearable blow of losing her, when that time should come to pass.

And he did—Zeek eased the blow just a little, though perhaps only by facilitating some sort of denial, just shifting all my focus toward being in love with him, when Camille passed away.

When Zeek did not return after chasing deer into the woods— when hunters came across his body not half a mile from our goat farm (they'd seen my "lost dog" fliers bearing Zeek's handsome likeness plastered for miles around)—now, **that** was when the unbearableness swooped in. When the pain of losing Camille and

Zeek both felt as though it would carry me away. It would cover me, like an avalanche. It would smother me until I was gone.

I tried to stave off the suffocation of loss with rescuing more dogs, rather than just grieving and focusing on little Joey (not to mention my goats, my horse, my cockatiel, and several rescued cats) for a while. Having scoured the Petfinder website for two months during Zeek's absence (hoping he would materialize in some random shelter or rescue), I was painfully aware of all the dogs who desperately needed homes. I adopted Luna without meeting her first—a big-eared black dog who looked like Camille, but could not have been more different in personality. Within weeks of my darling's body being found, I adopted a giant Great Dane/Hound mix, Logan, who reminded me somewhat of Zeek. Luna and Lo' were not at all good together, and I ended up eventually rehoming Logan to a loving family, who sent me photos of him for years. I'd decided to give Logan up only because I'd adopted Luna first, though in personality he was the better fit for me. It was an excruciating choice to make, and one I would question deeply. I don't believe it was the right choice for me. But so these things go, sometimes.

I was something of a wreck, still, when I decided to go to Colorado for the winter. I'd had my very first panic attack there in the springtime on a hike, when Logan nearly slid off a cliff.

All of the sadness, all of the loss. Distractions are only that, they do not take these feelings away.

I do not wish to wallow in misery, nor do I wish to deny the pain. Like my throbbing toe now as I rise and stretch (sending lighten bolts up through my foot), as I hobble to the back door to let Apollo inside. I want to just push through it, to walk as though it doesn't hurt—I want it not to hurt. I want all of the loss, all of the loneliness NOT TO HURT. I want all the fear to just not be there; like yesterday out on the trail, seeing that Great Pyrenees appear ahead of us, ambling toward us with no human in tow. It may as well have been a polar bear, for all the terror, the panic that rose in me to a fevered pitch. And I hated it—I hated being so afraid.

I want to be strong.
I do not want to be afraid.

"He's such a sweetheart," my friend would say to me later of the polar bear dog, after I'd scurried up a rocky hillside with my beloved Anzu snarling at the end of her leash—she wanted to kick that fluffy white dog's ass. I secured her to a tree with my running belt, brought the sproingy leash for the Pyrenees, whose name, his collar told us, was Ben. "You should pet him," my friend said.

I wanted to so badly, in my heart of hearts. I wanted to bury my face in the thick white mane of his scruff. I wanted to look deeply into those soulful eyes as they considered me curiously. I wanted to be seen, and feel SAFE.

Sweet Mother, all I want is to feel safe.

But no—he looked too much like the giant, beautiful dog who had sunk her teeth into the meat of my legs again and again and again. The part of my brain carrying that memory screamed too loudly, *NOT SAFE NOT SAFE NOT SAFE.*

"I would love to," I said to my friend as she crouched with Ben on the trail, "thank you. But not while I'm feeling so much fear." What broke my heart was that the dog could feel it, too; he could feel my fear, and it caused him to eye me suspiciously.

All these great lessons, these reminders from the Universe, from Spirit, from God, or whatever you want to call it. All these reminders, and (effing) opportunities for Growth. As my toe throbs this morning, and I laugh as I grimace in pain—the irony of this, as I'm supposed to go meet with the handsome personal trainer for our first work-out session this morning. Okay, Universe, Spirit, God, or whoever—what is my lesson in this? This must be a pretty good one.

I am breathing deeply, and keeping my humor about this, truly. I am smirking at the irony. I am practicing Not Pushing Any Rivers; I am moving deliberately, slowly, one acute step at a time. I am paying attention.

I am paying attention.

Deep breath in, and out.

Wednesday, November 3, 2021
5:23 a.m.

First things first.

Heal my Little Girl, teach her how to feel safe. That will be infinitely helpful toward the cause of helping the angsty teenager girl in me, and toward helping my grown-up self. Which will, of course, lead to helping me with Fisher, as well as helping meet the needs of other loved ones in my periphery. Which in turn will help support all others whose lives we may influence in this ongoing ripple effect.

Not yet noon.

Eating chickpea salad; Anzu listening from the dog bed for when I will be finished so she can lick out my bowl. Ashaya is sitting down to my right at the base of the wooden chair. She has just given her tiny left hind foot a very thorough licking, now lays her head down on the carpet, and begins to tremble. She sits up for a moment, gazes up at me with her sweet, buggy eyes, her bat-ears quivering. I meet her gaze for a moment, and smile. I go back to writing. She lays her tiny head back on the carpet and continues to shake.

This morning I found myself in quite a pickle, having fetched my two client dogs, gotten to the North Backbone Trailhead, finding two vehicles parked there—one, a white sedan crammed messily with the sorts of things which insinuate someone living out of it, possibly still sleeping in it at that moment. Visions of exuberant, collarless pit bulls emerging from the car went bounding through my head.

I feel exhausted just writing about it, though my vision did not manifest; my client dogs and I were safe, and had a good hike.

I feel over-filled with chickpeas.

I feel like it's time for me to check out for a little while, and I'm grateful that the time is nearly upon me. To set all these responsibilities momentarily aside. To have a day just for me.

I feel hopeful that the Journey tomorrow will help me find my way through all this burdensome fear.

I am hopeful for the rewiring,
for the recalibrating,
for the relearning and remembering.
I feel hopeful, ever so hopeful.
And right now, I feel really fucking tired.

Thursday, November 4, 2021
4:55 a.m.

At some point yesterday when the sun was setting, I took Anzu and Ashaya for a short walk in the field, figuring that after our busy day and their outing at the stable, a short walk would suffice. I had eaten too much, as I knew I had, in the curious state I was in—following old habits of eating too much, even though it makes me feel worse in the end.

I was in bed by 7 p.m., exhausted, and aware that Fisher would not be done with his drama club for another hour and a half; feeling so grateful that Ryan had agreed to pick him up at this late hour, beginning their two weeks together. So grateful that I just got to be in this state of exhausted weirdness, and not impose it on anyone else.

I woke up at 9 p.m. and thought, *My goodness—it's only nine.* Was having a really hard time sleeping, frustrated by the sounds of Ashaya licking herself beneath the covers (which makes me want to scream) and aware of all the light pouring in my bedroom window, even from the nightlight in the bathroom. Around 11 p.m. I got up to pee, and as I climbed back into bed, Ashaya hopped out to get a drink of water, then was reluctant to jump up on the bed again. I had the thought:

You need to make it darker in your room.

Then: *You need to love the little dog more.*

So I got up, turned off the night-light in the bathroom, and closed my blinds up tight. I lifted the little dog gently into bed, under the covers, and wrapped myself around her, kissing her sweet-smelling little head. My mind continued with its whirring, sometimes tugging me abruptly from half-sleep, but then...I felt a curious pressure on my back, like the touch of a gentle, soothing hand. Part of me did a quick assessment of possibilities, finding no earthly explanation for this sense. With that thought, I immediately felt soothed. My mind noted that maybe I should feel afraid, also noting that I did not—I felt comforted, deeply peaceful, and safe. So, wrapped around the form of tiny Ashaya in that state, I fell into a deep and peaceful sleep.

I may have roused briefly at 3 a.m. but woke up for sure at 4:30. Good, yes. Today is Journey Day, at the private cabin/ retreat center out among the forest and hills. I am ready. I am so grateful for this day.

* * * * * *

Another note from modern-day times: This has been an excruciating part for me to get into, which I guess is only telling me I've got more work around this to do. The insights gleaned in Journey Number Three—it is not the kind of thing where you just open up a can of worms, set them free, and never have to deal with them ever, ever again (thank heavens!). To the contrary, you open up that can of worms and set them loose in your garden… allowing their presence to feed and nurture your soil, let them encourage your vegetables to grow and your flowers to bloom.

Let those worms help set *you* free.

I will interpret my Journey notes as best as I can, taking deep breaths as I go.

* * * * * *

Third Medicine Journey
Thursday, November 4, 2021
MDMA

Intentions: To release fear, come into love/safety, release blockages, deepen connection with animals, attend to the little girl at the top of the stairs (by baby Wendy's room, my Protector also concerned about keeping her safe).

As the Journey notes outline, after our opening ceremonies, I took the medicine at about 10:00 a.m.

As the medicine set in, I began crying that I missed my Mom, as I have vocalized in the past. I began to experience a sense of forgiveness, feeling the presence of Nana, and Big Daddy (my father's dad), who was a very stern and intimidating fellow. I said that Big Daddy was just scared, too. "I know you loved me," I told him.

I remember laying there, feeling sort of far away, thinking that maybe the medicine wasn't really working. Then I began to get sort of a download from all the dogs in my present and recent history, beginning with Anzu—a download of all their trauma.

Anzu as a Reservation puppy, where dogs had to fight for resources to survive. Then she was taken from her momma, and was sick with parvo. She was frightened, and confused.

Ashaya in the hoarding situation she was rescued from, along with twenty-some other little dogs. The inches of feces they all had to live in, with some that did not survive, their bodies left to rot in the waste. Too many dogs, not enough food, and never, ever going outside...

Then came a download from Wren, a formidable King Shepherd I'd adopted about a year after the Pyrenees attack. He was an amazing, loyal, loving dog, who bonded to me quickly, but wanted me all for himself. When he'd been with us for about two good weeks, one day he jumped out the back of the Subaru and bee-lined for my old llama in the pasture—after giving chase, being spat on repeatedly and even kicked in the eye, he took my poor llama down to the ground, clutching the back of Sebastian's neck in his mighty jaws. I was bitten trying to pull Wren off. In the weeks after that incident, Wren and Anzu began getting into terrifying knock-down, drag-out fights, which I was next to useless for breaking up, due to a paralyzing fear of being bitten again. To my heartbreak, Wren had to go back to the shelter, where he was treated well, put on anti-anxiety meds, and eventually adopted to a fellow familiar with the huge breed and their needs, and who had no livestock around.

"Wren thought he was going to get supper, but llamas are not for supper," I told Joan, then went on, "I'm so sorry, Wren, baby. I'm so sorry you had to leave me. You're a good boy, and you were protecting me. I'm so sorry I couldn't keep you with us. Did you find your new daddy, Wren?" I turned to Joan. "Baby Wren went to a new place. He was my protector. We did the best we could...he didn't know." He didn't understand he had to share me with our other dogs, and that llamas are not to be eaten for supper.

Next came Aspen, the Pyrenees who attacked me. "Your mama was upset," I said of Aspen, "she was protecting her mama…" The dog was definitely picking up on her owner's stress, perhaps believing it was because of me. "It's okay, baby girl—you didn't know, sweet Aspen. She is beautiful," I said to Joan. "She did her best, too. I'm so sorry you were upset, Aspen. It's okay you bit me. It scared me having your teeth in my legs, but it's okay, you were just protecting your momma. I'm grateful because I can heal now…you're so good…"

Then I remember getting really, really tired.

The notes say I went inward, with Joan reminding me of my intentions. I remember her tapping some sort of tuning fork near my head. I started to laugh and to say, *That's the sound that the spaceship made when Momma and Light Momma took me away, away from my body and that place…*

But the words didn't come out—there was a *whoosh*—

—like sliding down a waterslide into memory, into trauma—

Then I began to sob. "I love you, baby. Honey—what do you need? Did somebody hurt you? Oh, baby girl…" Joan and I talked with my Protector inside, the one at the top of my childhood stairs with me. We thanked him, and reminded him that the little girl is safe now. "You can stay here, help me keep her safe," I said. "Where was Daddy? Did he go away? Who was the person who stayed?"

And I began to remember…the dreadful loneliness, the fear, the betrayal, the rage…

"That man wasn't safe," I began. "He was not safe to leave with three little girls…He was not okay. *That man was not okay…*" I began to writhe and to yell as sensations flooded my body. *"You get out of this house," I growled. "YOU GET OUT OF THIS HOUSE!"*

I called that man by his name.

Joan grabbed a pillow and leapt to the end of the sofa where I struggled; she held it up and told me to kick, to kick that man away—

I kicked and pushed, I hollered out loud, *"YOU GET OUT OF HERE! NO! NO!!!"*

You get out of this house—

I couldn't kick hard enough.

When I relayed the story to Brandi a couple of days later, she observed, "Of course you couldn't, you were just a little girl." That made perfect sense to me.

I don't remember exactly how things went after that, but it was definitely quite a release.

The Journey notes say I went outside, "connecting with" my body, the sunshine, and nature. I was barefoot, telling Joan it felt good. I remember being in the warm sun on the back deck looking at the garden, the trees, the mountains off in the distance. "Oh!" Joan exclaimed suddenly, leaping back indoors, "I know what we should listen to!" From inside the cabin, I heard the opening acoustic guitar notes to John Denver's song "Country Roads," and I began to sway, and sing, and smile, raising my hands to the trees and the sky. This song—a beautiful memory from my childhood, among the very few, of my dad singing with his deep, full voice, dancing with we girls. Joan emerged from the open back doors to the deck, and began to dance with me...

It was quite a blissful scene.

Soon after, we blew out the candle, closing ceremony.

There are more words I wrote at the end of the Journey notes Joan gave me:

"Walked out in the field, sat on stones by the fire circle. Lay in the sun on the deck, by the back doors open to the living room. Joan packed up to leave…Anzu followed her out to the car, and held her there for me…I became a little girl again, so sad—

Momma momma momma, don't leave—

Joan sees me, comes back up the stairs to the deck, saying, 'I know, this is a big trigger for you.' I curl in a fetal pose on the warm wood, crying. Joan comforts me. She asks if I would like her to come back for supper—I say through tears, 'Yes, please.'

She leaves, and I am fine there by myself, with the dogs and the birds, and the bunnies, with the woods and grass and mountains to keep me company…I remind myself that she will be back.

Two Journeys now that she has come back to stay with me.

By nighttime my internal Protectors are back online, and I feel ready to be alone. It feels good to have the place to myself in the morning, and I find myself not wanting to leave."

* * * * * *

Friday, November 5, 2021
10:40 a.m.

The challenging thing now is that I don't want to leave… though I don't know if it's challenging, actually, it just is what it is. Joan said I could stay here for as long as I like, but I don't know if she meant that literally, and I only brought provisions for one long day of Journeying, for one night and a morning—a morning that is slowly slipping away. I would be so very content to stay here all day long, curled up by the woodstove's crackling flame, Ashaya curled against my hip (there is no room in my lap with the journal poised there), eating potato chips and writing, watching the many birds pluck seeds from the tall flowers in the garden, now dormant.

When I first pulled in to this place through the trees, at the end of a meandering dirt road, I was amazed—it was like entering a magical realm. There was part of me which felt deeply saddened that I'd not jumped on the opportunity when it had first gone on the market through a realtor friend. It would be a perfect place for me and my animals, a perfect little Writer and Artist's retreat. It could have been amazing for me, had I been open and ready for it then, but, noh—the timing was not quite right. It would have been too soon to sell my new townhouse, and commit to the commute. The timing for me was just not right—so I'm grateful I told Joan about this place, and she bought it, instead of me.

1:40 p.m.

I still am not ready to leave this place, as the sun travels across the sky. The dogs have been watching me with curiosity as I move from one room to another, tidying and gathering my little things from here and there, moving them out to the kitchen, or to the chair by the picture window and wood stove. I have not napped yet, though I lay on Dyan's comforter on the back deck with Dad's pillow and Pooh-bear pillowcase beneath my head. I could have slept there, certainly, in the shade of the aspen and pine trees. But Anzu and Ashaya took to wandering around while I dozed, so I rose to wander out into the trees with them, instead. There is much gentle evidence of the twenty years spent here by the woman who built this house, the horse shelters and corrals, the clearings and meandering paths through the woods. Often they'll end abruptly in a small, open space, surrounded by a tiny forest of scrub oak, their leaves all brown with the coming of winter. Sometimes there will be a curiously placed or overturned large stone, beckoning for one's bum to rest there, so that the tiny dog may hop up to settle in your lap, to sit quietly, and listen, and breathe the crisp, mountain air. It is so quiet and peaceful here, smacking of wild turkeys and deer and the bear who pushed down the top of the wire fencing around the garden, scrunching it down just enough to get the hummingbird feeders hanging there. I wonder about that bear. I wonder about the bunnies, one of whom I saw hopping around by the truck earlier, down at the base of the grassy field, where surely wildflowers grow in the summertime. Did the woman who built this home by hand also seed that field, 'round the big fire pit in its center? Did she clear the trees to make that grassy space? Who was her dog who is buried up above the clearing, with so many rocks and a large dog collar? Was that dog a Great Pyrenees? Did he guard this land, and his momma? Is that his tie-out line I untangled from the bramble by the front porch? Did he sleep during snowstorms underneath that deck, as any Great Pyrenees might like to? If this were my place, I would have a Pyrenees, for sure. I would have the whole ten acres fenced in well, for him to patrol. I would have two llamas, and a small, sturdy horse, maybe two. I might make that old dog kennel down below into a super sturdy, bear-proof chicken coop. And the yard around the house would be securely fenced so Anzu and Ashaya and Manu could wander about, but I could still step out on the porch to always see them. I would install a beautifully elegant claw-foot bathtub, like the one at my Baker friend's country home in Wisconsin. I would make that little (tiny) guest house into a two-story loft, with a small deck below and one on top...what a lovely guest house it would make, or an Artist's studio. That is what I'd do, if this were my place. And most certainly there would be koi once again in that pond.

If not this place, some other magical place like it—these visions are dancing in my head. These are all such lovely ideas, and the feel of this place...it is a good reminder that these places do exist. The time was not right for us, when it came on the market; the time was just not right. But it is perfect for this—a place of healing journeys, and discovery, and retreat. And I am SO GRATEFUL to be here now for this. I am so grateful for the experience of yesterday, here in this magical place, with Joan, and Anzu, and Ashaya. And the birds tittering in the trees, the sun traveling warm across the sky...this time yesterday, I was laying on the floor in the doorway to the back deck, my bare feet high in the air, the sunshine warm upon my soles, my legs, my bum. This time yesterday I was beginning to slide gently down the other side of the slope from that peak, and I was very, very sleepy. I was beginning to worry a little about what time

Joan had to leave. And we blew out the candles, and we said our Thank Yous...

(Oh, momma, momma, please don't leave...)

And this stuff is super challenging, to say the least. And a friend sent me a beautiful song this morning that made me cry—and if you're crying then you're healing, he said. I told Brandi, I feel tender, like a healing wound.

I don't want to leave this place, and that's okay. I want to putter around and haul wood and read books. But Apollo and all the fish in the aquarium are waiting patiently for me at home, and my body is telling me it wants a huge, green salad.

So, take it easy on yourself, my darling. Take it gentle, take it slow. Be so careful with these tender wounds, that they may heal. Pack up your shrine with reverence, with sweetness, and care—I know you have been resistant to doing so. It's okay, it's alright, sweetheart—you are doing such a good job, you are doing such strong and important work. As you heal yourself, you may be in a position to help others heal themselves, too. You know this is true. And this place of healing is not going anywhere. Bless it, and thank it as you leave, with Love. Tell it you look forward to seeing it again soon.

Aw, sweet lil' baby girl.
Aw, there, darling—you are doing so good.

(Anzu sighs, laying in the sunshine in the living room.)
2:57 p.m.

5:12 p.m.

I remember being at the weeklong retreat in California—the one with the amazing food—in the big room, everyone sitting or kneeling with our large pillows in front of us, poised and ready to beat the crap out of said pillows with a baseball bat. We were instructed to vocalize, to really let 'er rip, and I remember when given the command to let loose, I startled myself with my own ferocity, screaming, *"MOTHER FUCKER—YOU DO NOT DO THAT TO LITTLE GIRLS!!!!"*

Um, excuse me?

Was I talking to Daddy for hitting us? For being emotionally unavailable, and working so much, and for leaving us alone? For being angry and broody, for going into rages, or retreating behind closed doors, to where we couldn't get to him...is that what I was so venomous about?

Or was it something more insidious than that?

I cannot remember now how that all went in my Journey yesterday, and there is a part of me that does not want to—it feels like daggers in my chest. Am I just making this up as some horrific fairytale of my childhood, or is this unthinkableness actually real? I feel like throwing up just bringing these images to my mind, at the Bagley Parkway house...down in the basement. Up at the top of the stairs, when Daddy went away. Where did he go? Why wasn't he there to protect us?

I think it was when he went to Jamaica with his Farrah Faucette-looking girlfriend...the one who always seemed more important to him than me (even if this was only my perception, not truth). That would make sense, that that was when. So much horrific sense.

Am I just making this up? Is this some crazy drug-induced nightmare I am concocting? It feels surreal, yet is burning in my chest. No—put it away—I don't want to look at that. I don't want these horrific images in my mind.

As my body shook and trembled feverishly yesterday, as my teeth chattered and Joan held me tightly, echoing my words, asking me what else I wanted to say...

NO—*THAT IS NOT OKAY.*

NO—*YOU DON'T DO THAT TO LITTLE GIRLS.*

NO. NO. NO—

YOU GET OUT OF THIS HOUSE.

What
the living fuck.

Driving up the canyon towards home, these words echoed in my head. I began talking to myself out loud, soothing the little baby girl who was crying, she was so scared and alone. "It's okay, baby girl, it's okay. You're alright, we're just driving home. No one's going to hurt you, baby girl, it's okay, you're safe. It's okay, baby girl, you're safe."

Back at the townhouse, my mind tries to unpack all the images, the feelings, all the puzzle pieces throughout my lifetime, trying to make sense of this...to make sense of what is senseless.

It's okay, baby girl, it's okay, you're safe. You're in your daddy's home now, baby girl. You are in YOUR HOME—you are in your home, now, and you're SAFE.

Chapter 16
Love = Release

"It's all lies.
Back to Nature,
the only truth."

—Rick Rubin, to Andrew Huberman

So, yes.
That was all a lot.

And, truly, that was just the beginning of so much more to unfold...You wouldn't even believe me if I told you all of the Everything. Or maybe you would—and maybe I will one day. But for right now, that is enough. With three Journeys down, and so many insights unfolding, so many neural pathways being rebuilt. It would continue to feel really hard for some time, what with all of the trauma dug up. There was an awful lot to process with the help of my spirit guides, with the help of good counselors, with the help of insightful and compassionate family and friends. And also...it is amazing—truly remarkable—how my inner strength began to rebuild itself, how I began to mend. After all of that, and always with the sensation of moving three steps forward and two steps back, I absolutely began to mend.

I began to stand in my Power, with uncanny certainty.

I began to manifest the life I'd seen in my dreams, in my mind, and in my journalings.

My realtor friend who'd told me about the cabin which became the retreat center two years earlier started sending me photos one morning last spring, saying, "This place has Laura written all over it!" When I reluctantly decided to just go "check it out," I was amazed. I stepped out onto the back deck overlooking a forest complete with a snow-fed mountain creek and majestic, rising peaks. It had the same magical feel as the cabin I'd fallen in love with on my third Journey, that nurturing place I had not wanted to leave. Here was this place now, available to me. And down in the backyard, among all the alpaca fencing and loafing sheds and trees, was a giant, beautiful, terrifying Great Pyrenees.

"You should come pet her," Fisher called to me, his hands through the fence on the dog. "She's super sweet."

That time I would not. The sound of her bark at a passing truck on the road still made fear rise up in me, burning hot all the way to my ears. But on our second visit to the homestead, I stood near this glorious polar bear of a dog, with only a fence between us. By the third visit, I petted her, and asked if she could come with the house. So, this is how we came to Ivy, and how Ivy came to us. This is how my dream unfolded in fits and starts, in hesitations and miraculous unfoldings which no one could have foretold, because every time it seemed there was no way this was going to happen—this buying of my dream farm—the stars aligned, and another doorway opened, ushering me along. Right down to Lee coming up from Arizona to cosign the home loan with me, declaring simply, "That's what Family does for each other." Right down to Lee and Beorn stepping up nobly to move me out of the townhouse and onto this farmstead—to get the house into an inhabitable state—even as I felt completely overwhelmed, like collapsing into puddles of snotty tears, and questioning my own freakin' sanity. Until here I am, sitting at my mother's antique kitchen table, a fire crackling in the woodstove. Darkness cloaks slumbering mountains outside the windows all around my home, where I watch the moon travel across the night sky. Where the sunrise filters in golden every morning across the open living area to my kitchen, illuminating my wooden cabinets as though offering warm spotlights, compelling them to burst into song...though usually I'm the one singing and dancing. Where I breathe in deeply, awestruck, amazed. Where I marvel at how surreal it all feels sometimes, these miracles unfolding around me.

And I don't want to be too airy-faerie about it, because I still have challenges, to be sure. I still have my bouts with melancholy, doubt, ennui, and fear. I still have conflicts with Fisher sometimes, which both of us find triggering, to say the least—though I must pause here to gush about what an amazing young man he's becoming, navigating his own brilliant awareness through strong self-work, leaving me in awe of his wisdom and maturity. I still grapple with loneliness, and my addictive leanings toward cute boys (read: beautiful men; desire for the respect and adoration I craved from my father) and chocolate, both of which can make me feel like a crazy person. I managed to find myself a magical, musical mermaid muse for a while, who stoked flames of passion and creativity in me. He lived just far enough away—away off in the sea, one might say—to remain not entirely real to me.

I still try sometimes to placate my Big Feelings with food, which might offer momentary relief. I am still making peace with these parts of myself who struggle, losing their balance, forgetting what they've learned and the resources available to them. Those parts who get frightened, angry, needy, or self-deprecating. Those parts who can lash out defensively at ones dearest to them. Those parts who require nurturing, or just want something delicious in their mouth (and I do not always mean food). Those parts who need to be cooed to, caressed, to be kissed, sometimes passionately. To be held firmly, calmly, and reassured with utmost certainty, that all will be well in the end.

I had three more Journeys over the span of a year or so after my third, the one that completely shook my world. Every Journey has had its own theme and has been part of the broader progression of insight, and shifting, often in brilliant ways I never could have foreseen. The rebuilding of what had collapsed into an unsettled foundation. The repairs are being made, meticulously. When the foundation is strong, by golly, the structure may be built upon with purpose and intention; it may rise in full glory toward the sky.

My last Journey was here at the farmhouse, on a cool, rainy day, with the French doors flung open wide to the back deck, the mountains, the babbling creek, the birds, the trees. What I remember most about that day was lying on the floor with the dogs all around me, a fire crackling in the woodstove. I remember sobbing, and singing, and leaving my body, again and again…going out into the ether where there were the Spirits, and God…then coming back into my body again, and sobbing. It was so hard to be in this body, on this Earth. There is so much pain and confusion here, so much upheaval and unrest. So, I would leave my body again, back out to the liberation of the spirit world, of LIGHT. Of pure and unadulterated Love. And the Spirits would ask me, "Do you want to go back into your body again, Love? Or would you like to stay out here a while longer?" When I'd return to my body, there was so much pain there, so many unresolved traumas from my past, and also—there was Ivy. I was laying on her, my head pressed to her chest, my arms around her, sobbing, writhing, grasping her thick polar bear fur. I found soothing in the sounds of her heartbeat, of her breath. Apparently, she lay there with me for the entire five-plus hours. My guide told me later that none of the four dogs moved, except to remain near me, often pressed to my body. Not a one of them asked to go outside, nor so much as left the room throughout my entire Journey.

And the Spirits cooed to me, "There you go, darling…" They went through my entire body, piece by piece. They illuminated every trauma, every awful memory I was holding, every sad or horrific thing that had ever happened to me, and they'd say, "There you go, darling—are you ready to release this piece? Or would you like to hold on to it a little longer?" They asked me that again and again. I still hear them asking me now. They were so kind, and patient, and nurturing to me, as I sobbed that I missed living with them out in the ether, that being in a body is so hard.

And it all makes sense to me, why I'd lost connection with my body, in all of its pain. Why, when Momma and Light Momma helped me leave my body when I was a little girl, when it was being hurt, I never felt safe going fully back into my body again.

So, can you allow yourself to feel safe now in your body, little girl? Or do you need to stay out a while longer?

This, this, this. This is the question I feel shimmering in my bones. This is the question I think so many earthbound humans grapple with. Of how to feel truly safe, and loved, and loving in these vessels of clay. When truly we are beings born to be unbound.

That time, on the floor surrounded by my loving pack of dogs, I chose to go back into my body, eventually. I understood that this is my choice, and that I have work to do here in this realm. That the work is never done, per se. It is a gloriously ever-present evolution.

* * * * * *

Saturday, December 23, 2023
5:40 a.m.

Yesterday became a day of so much internal struggle for me, so much freaking out. So much stirring things up with my mermaid muse, not content to just let things lay where we'd left them, compelled to ask him again and again, *What was the shift that happened a week ago? Why did the energy change?* Pushing and pushing and wanting to understand a greater depth to something, where there was no greater depth which ultimately required understanding. Ultimately, this is not about *him.* Allow the truth to be as he told me—that right now he needs to focus on himself and his creative goals—a concept I fully understand. Sometimes things just go this way…and they can go the other way, too.

Yet my compulsions, my addictions, my insecurities rise to push me out of balance again, snarling, *"No, no, no–"* As they slide me off my base with strong, hairy arms and gnarled fingers and terrible morning coffee breath. *"No, no, no–! You need to find the* things, *the* people *OUTSIDE of yourself to reassure you that you're strong, and pretty, and capable, and good! You **need** this beautiful mermaid muse to keep reminding you: It is as he told you early on, exactly so, that **you deserve nothing less**."*

Ah. Yes.
This, again.

I found myself reaching out to Beorn, asking if he had any insights for me. Telling him I didn't want to keep doing what I did to him, so what should I be doing differently? I didn't want to lose my muse with all my pushing, incessantly.

Beorn replied, "I would say do exactly as you did with me. NONE of why we aren't together has to do with you."

I paused. My heart felt all a' jumble. I texted, "Why is that making me cry?"

He responded with a shoulder-shrugging emoji.

Beorn acknowledged feeling hurt so badly in his past, it made him emotionally unavailable. "Obvious, I suppose, but I'm finally working on it with a therapist."

It was like clouds opened up in my darkened sky, allowing a brilliant light to shine through. I swear I heard angels sing.

Now, I close my eyes. I take a deep breath through my nose.

I sit up straight in the creaking wooden chair, which was my father's, the sound of which time-travels me back to childhood when I was small and frightened, and also—the sound from away off behind closed doors, the sound that meant Daddy was there.

Time-travel forward, darling—to this moment where you sit at your father's desk, tall and strong. Where each creak of the chair makes you smile at the marvel of how far you have traveled in this body, on this Earth, to bring you to where you are right now: fire blazing in the wood stove behind you, glorious animal family all around you.

And my addictions, my compulsions, my insecurities—my demons—let them be embodied in forms that I may have compassion for. Let me take their gnarled fingers gently, even as they are pushing me. Let me whisper to them soothingly, "No, no, no, my darlings—it's alright. Come with me, back to Center. Come sit with me in this place of balance, of gratitude, of grace."

Let me breathe deeply, and kiss their contorted faces. Let me wipe away their tears. Let me thank them for how they have tried to protect me ever since I was a little girl, when it was Momma's time to leave her body. When Daddy was left angry, and sad, and scared.

"Look, my darlings," let me tell them, "Look how far we've come! Look at where we are right now, with the forest and the mountains outside our windows, with the noble guard llama and a couple horned goats in our yard. Look—it's alright, and I've got you! Look now, darlings—we are safe."

This safety which comes from within—
When we are connected with the All and the Everything.

It can feel challenging to reside in these bodies, to be sure. It can take some doing to remember our Divinity. But that will never make our Divinity any less present, or real. Just as the sun doesn't go away in the nighttime, or when obscured by looming clouds. The truth is always present, as the sun continues to blaze warmly, with more power and glory than can be conceived of by our brains made of spongy meat and firing neurons. It is something we perhaps only fully grasp when unshackled from these bodies—through music, through massage, through writing, through meditation, through orgasms, through medicinal journeys, or simply through our dreaming...All the times when we leave our bodies, however fleeting these experiences may seem.

Then back into its Center, my spirit nestles—this light which is the essence of Me. Settle back into this body, the gift of this lifetime, sitting tall on this creaky chair, in this moment, NOW.

After all my flopping around (energetically speaking) like a fish out of water, after laying crumpled on the floor and sobbing to Brandi over the phone about how I push and push, how it pushes love away from me...and have I not learned *anything*? She tells me, with such compassion in her tone, that she understands it feels that way, and also, she has *seen me come SO FAR.*

Finally, after all of that was out and done, the voices whispered gently, "There you go—feel better now? Are you ready to come back to Center?" A feeling wrapped around me, warm like a blanket. A feeling of calm, and peace, and purpose. I turned on my computer, sat down at the kitchen table, which was my mom and dad's before I was a sparkle in their eye. I opened the journal to where I'd left off—after Journey Number Three. The one which served as the lancing of a festering wound, letting out all the toxic, wretched mess I'd been carrying for most of my life, unconsciously informing my every thought, my every move. The RELEASE of it all—let it Out, let it Go. Let it be cleansed, and purified by the healing warmth of sunlight on that deck by the cabin in the woods.

And I was amazed. Even as I felt resistance to diving back into that painful time and all that was brought to light in my third Journey, the words of comforting written back then sunk into me now, perhaps even more deeply than they'd been able to sink in before, when I was raw, and open, and hurting. Now that I've had time to tend those wounds, to build my strength anew, without those toxins of trauma festering inside of me. Now that I've been able to experience the navigation of Life with tools I'd not been fully conscious of sooner...of what it looks like to be pushed off-balance and to seek support, rather than succumbing to despair. Where that support can come from in its myriad sources; through Spirit, through spirits, through trusted friends and confidants. Through the animals, and through nature, always. By breathing deeply in through my nose, then another quick breath deeper still, then RELEASING with vigor from the mouth (in what we'll just call the "Huberman Sigh," henceforth). Through the infinite resources available to me, if only I can take a moment to pause, and remember, and allow myself to feel it in my chest, in my body, in my very bones—this light which is in every fiber of me. In every fiber of All of Us, and in Every Thing. A moment in stillness, silence, and gratitude, to remember—

That for every darkness, there is a light.
For every down there is an up.
That this is our opportunity for **experience,** this Life.
That we have the power, the strength in every moment...

to **choose.**

* * * * * *

It behooves me to address, in no uncertain terms, that the Medicine Work is a powerful tool, not to be wielded with frivolity. In every single Journey undergone, I've vocalized at some point (usually as the medicine begins to fully take hold) that "I can't imagine doing this recreationally." Obviously, there are those who do, and certainly everyone has to make their own decisions on all matters, always. I also acknowledge that long ago it was me dabbling around with that curiosity...but at this stage of my work, I can't imagine it. Not to mention that it seems to me a bit like poking a sleeping dragon with a stick—an endeavor not to be acted upon without significant forethought and intentionality.

It is also important to be aware that even highly monitored psychedelic therapies are not going to be helpful for everyone. I know of instances where it has been downright harmful for some, leading to profound unease, to psychotic breaks, and even schizophrenia—perhaps having triggered a predisposition to the disorder. There are some for whom it may simply stir up so much muck that it becomes difficult to function in day-to-day life. My hope for those is that their intentional work will continue (with or without the use of psychedelics, but certainly with professional support), and that even the intense discomfort of what the medicines reveal to them will be helpful in their healing, eventually.

For myself, the continuing one-on-one therapy with a counselor has been crucial in my processing between Journeys. I have never done a Medicine Journey without a counselor present to oversee, to guide me when appropriate, and to make sure that I am safe. So, you know—that's just me. And, of course, for me, the presence of animals has always been crucial—I have been blessed to have my dogs around me for every single Journey. Also, being in nature, having access to fresh air, to rocks, and gardens and trees—this has been integral to the healing process for me. To have earth to slam my fists upon as I sob and wail and scream. To have a large, warm rock I can lay my body over, thanking it for taking my pain from me. This has been so much of my healing.

In an interview on the Huberman Lab Podcast, Dr. Anna Lembke, author of *Dopamine Nation*, expressed her take on Psychedelic Assisted Psychotherapy as a gondola ride to the top of a mountain, forgoing crucial stages of the mountaineering experience. I truly admire Dr. Lembke, and I understand and concur with her analogy, to a degree. I believe we all have profound wisdoms deep within us, and can access them with practice, training, and diligence—even if we never reach the top of the mountain until we have an epiphany of Unconditional Love on our death beds. However, while psychedelics may not be entirely necessary for this ascension process, at this stage of human evolution, it seems it could be helpful, considering the brevity of our human lifespan, and the chaos we've been wreaking upon each other and our beautiful planet. I believe if we're going to stand a chance of undoing damage done, we're really going to need to step up the momentum of awareness, insight, and healing, both personally and globally. We've got to get a whole bunch more folks onboard (ASAP) with the whole freakin' Love and Light thing, and with the whole thing of seeing Everything and Everyone as connected, symbiotically. We need to start truly considering the ultimate well-being of absolutely EVERYONE and EVERYTHING.

We're running out of time here, folks. Really.

For me, personally, the work goes on. The story and the evolution continue.

I met with my beautiful butterfly friend not long ago; it had been a while, and we had some catching up to do about the paths we've been on, and what we are learning. I told her that I felt like the book was almost done, and, as a writer, she asked me how I knew. I told her I'd decided just to rein it in after the third Journey, and that was enough for now. We agreed we could both go on writing forever.

"Well, yeah, because this is the ongoing journey of *Life*," I said to her. "I mean, *really*. Fuck."

We burst out laughing, and heartily agreed—that should be the end to the story.
For now, at least, in this ongoing Journey.

I mean, really.
Fuck.

In Closing

"If I lose the light of the sun,
I will write by candlelight, moonlight, no light.
If I lose paper and ink, I will write in blood on forgotten walls.
I will write always. I will capture nights all over the world
and bring them to you."

—Henry Rollins

August 22, 2022

Time marches on, the curious configuration of realities we construct through our own perceptions, our own creations. Tick, tick, tick, the moments roll by. The sun begins to rise, way over there beyond the hills to the east. The kitten cries, lonely now that Apollo is outside, and I have ensconced myself in the master bedroom (I am the Master, after all, of this grand townhouse). The morning is cool and crisp out there. A haze of moisture veils the mountains off to the west. This dream I am living. Coffee, soft light of morning. Sitting at my great-grandmother's desk, a book to my right which was my father's (I remember opening it when it lived in what was his guest room upstairs), a photo of me as a little girl to my left; with shoelace untied, a half worm in my muddy, delicate hand. The quote I've long found endearing taped to my wall, from my friend, Timothy, who passed now how many years ago? The years seem to fly by. "I love you and miss you because you are so pretty, and because you have so much tallness and kindness," Timothy wrote. I could say the very same to him. In this moment, these times, these realities all converge. Here. Now. Shift my focus, and in the next moment they may all slip away.

Do you remember, my darling, when you came out to Colorado for the winter? Do you remember that you intended to write a book? Do you remember that you weren't so sure what that book was going to look like, only that it had something to do with love, and self-discovery? It had something to do with the animals, and fear. It had something to do with finding peace and purpose in all of this. It had something to do with magic, and the weaving of all the great mysteries of life.

Do you remember, dear girl?

And everything is unfolding perfectly, because at the time your great story was to fall in love with the mountains and the wintertime (and a tattooed boy, and his feisty little dog, too). To create a new life in human form, instead. Ah, yes, I remember. I remember the smells and the feelings and the songs of the time. Now the life who wished to be brought into this world, now he's growing up tall, and beautiful, and strong. I hear his bed creaking upstairs, above my head, in what was once my father's guest room. I hear the boy rise, stride with giant feet and long limbs to the bathroom. I hear the water turn on, and sounds of his giant boy form shifting in the tub. This is the story, continuing. This is my Colorado Adventure unveiling itself further every day. This is a tale of action, of romance, of mystery, of intrigue. This is all the magic and the animals, and the learning as we go. This is the convergence of all the many influences and realities. This is the breathing in of this moment, and giving thanks. This is the next moment, breathing out and marveling, as that moment slips away.

* * * * * *

THE END
(Bwah-hah-ha-ha-ha!!)

ACKNOWLEDGEMENTS

First of all, allow me to acknowledge that angels come in endless sizes, forms, and species. When I am truly paying attention (and not completely distracted by being tangled up in human concerns) I recognize them all around me. In the face of that dog. In that blade of grass. In the voice of the road crew worker who blesses me with his bidding, "drive safe."

With that being said and even so, for whatever reasons, I find this last little bit of my book difficult to complete. Perhaps it is because it feels like such an important thing to do, to fulfill the expression of my gratitude in a way as to honor its enormitude. Yes, I just made that word up, but really, you know what I mean, right? I want my words to be eloquent and clear. To ring poetic, yet not contrived. I want those who read this to understand how truly freakin' over the moon grateful I am for all of them—for the words, for the people—for all of it, and everything. So much so that I don't know where to begin.

What an incredible experience this has been and continues to be, this creation of a Book. It began with the first diary my dad bought for me when I was in the third grade; I opened every entry with "Dear Diary," which I now recognize as writing letters to the Divine, as well as to the divine I did not yet realize resides within me. Words were to become my greatest counsel throughout my lifetime, the writings my greatest confidante. The opportunities for unabashed introspection deepened my appreciation for humans, animals, the natural world, and eventually for myself—all as divine creation.

I feel awash with gratitude as my editor, Laura Thomas, picks up the phone, and I hear her baby boy making baby boy noises through the receiver. She seems delighted to hear from me, listens intently to my quandary, her caring voice illustrating the epitome of eloquence and clarity—that which my own mind and voice desire. She draws me from near tears into laughter, assuring me I can do whatever I want. I can NOT write Acknowledgements at all, or I can just make a list of bullet points, if I like. It's all up to me, she reminds me, soothingly. Through the telephone I can almost see the sparkles in her eyes—the same cloud of sparkle-dust she seems to walk around in all the time. The optimism and reassurance she has sprinkled around me since we first met many years ago, back when I shared with her that I moved to Colorado to write myself a book. It is Laura who referred me to the Journey Institute Press, my publisher, for which I feel tremendous gratitude. They took me under their wing upon Laura's good word and a Zoom interview, which began with Michael Jenet and I talking about dogs for the first several minutes of our conversation, a sure sign they were the Publishing Company for me. I am infinitely grateful for them giving me a chance with my first book. They had no idea what a pain in the arse my formatting would turn out to be...I do hope their perseverance will feel worthwhile to them in the end.

What magical creatures this creative process has brought to me, what friendships it has helped to forge. From way back to my days at Malcom Shabazz City High School, and the loving guidance of teachers like Henry Hawkins, Kristy Larson, and Kate Conklin (who stealthily submitted my poetry to writing competitions, yielding the first public affirmations of my word-craft). To all the creatives throughout my lifetime whom I've written about, and sometimes read to. All who were drawn to my colorful, dramatic nature, who seemed to appreciate me for my authenticity even through the uncomfortable bits. There were those who pulled me out of my self-conscious insecurities (all my bumblings with being human) by loving me with no strings attached. Taffy Hunder, Sarah Bailey, Tim Pfeiffer, Robbie Irish (whose declaration to Tim late one night I found endearing in its intent: "You're not supposed to ask her if she's okay!" he hollered. We all sure love and miss you, Tim). Jason Shaw and his dearest Canis, who loved me through all my tenderness and ferocity in my twenties, helping shape me into the Amazon Warrior I saw reflected in their eyes. Michiel Lofton, who became my closest friend and adventure partner for many, many years, influencing me deeply with the cutting-edge wit, humor, and cool bravery displayed in both his actions and his writing. Donn Jacobs and Toby LaFrancois—those guys were my super-steadies toward the end of Highschool, and for years to come. For all their playful shenanigans, I always knew how much they loved me and Camille, and (yes, Tobes) her beautiful little dog feet, too. Robert Armstrong, who first gave reason and permission for me to dive full-on into my creative passions, my weirdness, my emotional upheaval, and bliss. Cate Kuelbs and Josh (Wajid) Jenkins, among my intimate group of best-besties in High School, with whom I felt safe and supported unconditionally—a sensation I still carry in their presence to this day. Cate, it is difficult for me to express my depth of relief at the insights and reassurances you have offered me through this whole heart-cracked-wide-open process. Seriously, dude. Thank you for getting me.

My Arizona adventures created a chosen family for me among the cacti and desert valley, folks who I totally rocked-out with, and began growing a better version of myself. Melinda Xavier (who found my beloved Camille where she'd gone looking for me at an art fair near our home, instead bringing this lion-hearted woman to me), Dineen Serpa (Nee-nee-nee!), Jenni Shawkey (Aaa-ooo-gah! I know you can hear me way out there in the ether), Patrick (the mysterious, who first read me The Little Prince, and works by Kahlil Gibran, tolerating my blasphemy as I interrupted, laughing, "Defeat, my stinky defeat!"), Bret Lang, Jennifer Joyce, and of course, there was Lee Noble Street...

Lee deserves a paragraph all to himself as prime example of an Angel in the Flesh. He deserves gleaming trophies to gather dust upon his shelves, and gaudy medallions to hang 'round his neck (though he has far too much style for that)—and not just for how he's been of support to me. Lee is one of the kindest, big-hearted, generous and empathetic people I have ever known. I literally could not have written this book without him, as I very well could have thrown in the towel after my last computer crashed and burned. This is another one of those big huge things that words are ill equipped to express.

Now my brain is zipping and zooming through time, as it has a tendency to do. Through all the places and people and experiences for whom I am grateful, even the ones who maybe didn't pan out in ways I thought I wanted them to. It has all led me to where I am today, all freakin' awash in my gratitude... For the Tenny Family—Kathy, Kent, and Erin—who took me in when I was a teenager feeling unseen by my own blood relations; they taught me about sobriety and the tenets of AA. They taught me about healthy introspection and self-care, living naturally, creatively, authentically—even when that gets uncomfortable, or ugly. They gave me what felt like a safe place to come home to, which I did again and again. They introduced me to the likes of Jonathan Wilde, who just last winter counseled me over the phone, "Well, you're an artist, Laura. Why don't you do your own book cover?" Convincing me that not only do I have it in me, but that it would hold greater value. So, yep—Thank you, Jon.

Zip-zoom through time to all the mother figures I have been blessed to know, offering their strength, grace, and nurturing feminine energies. They became the powerful role models I desired as a young and motherless child. Marsha Cervetti Peterson, Margaret Schreiber, Joan Murphy, Susan Ellis, Jane Whitmer, and Dyan Steenport (with whom my relationship truly blossomed as a young woman after she was no longer married to my dad).

Zip-zoom out to the Rocky Mountains, and the family which drew me here—to my beloved sisters, Ginny and Wendy, with whom I share both heart and history. I am deeply indebted to you both for all we have experienced together, and for your love and support along this ongoing journey. We share a unique loving bond between sisters, like no other.

My gratitude extends to the welcoming mountains, becoming my home for the past two decades. The small-town (and growing) community has been nurturing and endurance-building, holding one to a warranted degree of accountability. If you've got someone here who you're uncomfortable with, you'd better make peace with it, because you're going to see them everywhere. For the most part, though, especially as somewhat of a hermit who has a tendency to just hunker-in with her animals, I am very grateful for the familial feel of the community among these mountains—for the friendly faces I come upon at Bunny and Clyde's Corner Café. For the clever banter and good humor I find waiting for me at the Library. For the calm, pleasant figures I see strolling around the Farmer's Market on a Saturday. Truly this place can be a soothing balm, and it has introduced me to people with whom I've appreciated the greatest integrity. Case in point: I could not possibly be more grateful for Ryan O'Brien, the father of our son. His integrity and commitment have shined through even the darkest of times, supporting not only Fisher's best interest but also my own, fully honoring the fact that unless we are all supported, the whole thing falls apart. I commend him on his willingness to get to the bottom of what the "needs" are in any given situation. I could not be more appreciative of the gracious and loving intentions of that man's heart.

Then there is our magical, musical boy, now nearly full-grown into a man. There is no way I could have foreseen the ferocity with which I would adore him, nor the urgency his very existence would put upon my need to better myself and to grow. I am grateful for the influence of his creativity, his enthusiasm, and the goodness of his soul. My darling Fish, I adore you with the infinite expansiveness of the Universe—I cannot imagine what my life would be like without the intoxicating luminescence of You.

These mountains also brought me the likes of Brandi Blade, who I dare say has grown with me in leaps and bounds, even as we've watched our babies grow into young men. I am grateful for the ways she loves me with bold curiosity and powerful tenderness. I am inspired by the ways I see her step into the fullest experiences of her own life. I appreciate the ways she can ask me the really difficult questions, then listen with her whole being to my well-considered replies. I love the way all my parts are welcome and beautiful to Brandi, even the most uncomfortable parts.

To feel truly accepted, appreciated, welcomed and embraced—this can be the greatest gift. Jill Flodstrom, I thank you for your healing strength and courage as such a needed presence in my life. To feel trusted and offered the same vulnerability in an honest exchange—Betsey McLaughlin, I thank you for exploring with me how to meet in the ineffable power of learning to Trust.

My sincere gratitude goes out to Kristen Moeller and David Cottrell, who have shared their home, their hearts, and their dogs with me. Kristen, you were such a motivator for me to continue with my writing, for every piece I shared which you expressed heartfelt appreciation for. As you say, we are just two little girls finding our way through this dance of life...there's a whole lot to it, that's for sure. Even when things get messy, I am so grateful for you loving me, and for allowing me to love you, too. Let's go find our Princess dresses and ponies, and get back out there together.

I seriously could keep going with this...but for sure cannot wrap it up without acknowledging the creatives who I do not know personally, but have influenced my endeavors profoundly. Oh, my goodness, the ways music moves me (I was reminded just yesterday of how Ocie Elliot's "Down by the Water" takes me back to the swooning beauty parts of my sixth Journey every time I hear it, often bringing tears to my eyes). Oh, my goodness, the experiences I have lived through the lenses of filmmakers, through the glorious words of authors and poets. The connection and comradery I have felt through the conversations of podcasters...folks like Rich Roll, Tim Ferris, and Andrew Huberman have influenced my thinking, feeling, and lifestyle choices with their cornucopia of nutrient-dense food for thought. It may sound strange, but they've come to feel like friends I just haven't met yet, though they join me in my kitchen for enlightening conversations every week.

Let us take a deep breath, finally, and settle in to the Here, to the Now. There are more people (and many animals) I could mention, who have motivated and supported me in beautiful and most appreciated ways. I will sincerely hope that You Know Who You Are.

At this stage of writing, it feels most important, dear reader, that I pause to acknowledge You. For being here, for witnessing my words. With utmost heartfelt sincerity, I thank you—for blessing me with your time, your attention, your consideration, and your care.

You are among the angels all around me, around all of us—don't you ever forget it, I beg of you. Keep using your powers for Good, my darlings.

Seriously.

Thank You.

ABOUT THE AUTHOR

Laura Holloway has been called Goat Girl, Animal Queen, and a Warrior Poet; semi-feral, fierce, and unabashedly "sensitive." She lives amidst the forest outside a small mountain town in Colorado, where she spends most of her time cleaning up after companion animals, frolicking through the woods, scribbling in her journals, and puttering around the farmstead sanctuary, daydreaming about butterflies and other magical beasts. She loves long walks in the woods with her pack of dogs, goats, llama, and the occasional enthusiastic cat, and never worries about looking like a total dork to her super-cool teenaged son. Laura aspires to master (and write about) the Art of Truly Loving Herself (really and for real), as well as loving this whole weird, wonderful world of whack-a-doodle Humanity. She also intends to lay off the chocolate, and to not take in any more cats. "Dancing with Demons: A Love Story" is her first proper book.

JOURNEY INSTITUTE PRESS

Journey Institute Press is a non-profit publishing house created by authors to flip the publishing model for new authors. Created with intention and purpose to provide the highest quality publishing resources available to authors whose stories might otherwise not be told.

JI Press focusses on women, BIPOC, and LGBTQ+ authors without regard to the genre of their work.

As a Publishing House, our goal is to create a supportive, nurturing, and encouraging environment that puts the author above the publisher in the publishing model.

Storytellers Publishing is an Imprint of Journey Institute Press, a division of 50 in 52 Journey, Inc.

NOTE: The world of publishing has changed dramatically. This has also affected authors and their ability to let readers know about their books. Today, most people buy books based on word of mouth.

If you would like to help this author, please consider leaving an honest review of this book on retail sites and book community sites.

THE
JOURNEY p
INSTITUTE
P R E S S